Dorothy Gates

Making Loose Covers and Cushions

with illustrations by the author

HAM PUBLISHING COMPANY LTD
Ellan Vannin, Droghadfayle Park, Port Erin, Isle of Man

First published by Frederick Warne in 1985
This edition published in 1988

British Library Cataloguing-in-Publication Data available.

ISBN 1 871235 10 3

Printed by Short Run Press Ltd., Exeter

Contents

To my dear sister and brother-in-law,
Rose and Barry

Equipment
Sewing machine
Piping foot
Zip foot
Large sharp scissors
Sharp steel pins approx. 3.25 cm. ($1\frac{1}{4}$ ins.)
Assorted sewing needles
Tape measure
Metre stick or yard stick
Tailor's chalk
Pencil
Note pad
Table with square edge

Materials
Fabric according to item
Lining for kick pleats or frill
Matching thread (40 gauge)
Piping cord
Zip
Button moulds
Touch and close tape
Lace
Ribbon
Insertion lace
Cushion pad
Braid

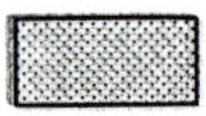 right side of fabric

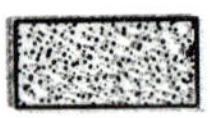 wrong side of fabric

Important note
Metric conversions are approximate. Make sure you use either all-metric or all-imperial measurements; do not mix the two.

Introduction

To cover the whole range of loose covers would be impossible in a book of this size. I have therefore chosen three types of furniture to include as wide a range of skills as possible. If you have some experience of cutting and sewing even the wing chair will not be too difficult, especially if you attend classes with a good tutor and have plenty of patience.

If you are going it alone, however, choose the easier project first so that you may gain confidence in the cutting.

The cutting out is the most important part of the whole cover as, if this is not done carefully and accurately, the finished item will look sloppy, however well you sew it. Very sharp scissors are essential for good loose-cover cutting and your pins must be sharp-pointed, a good average size being 3.25 cm. ($1\frac{1}{4}$ ins.). The turnings should be cut with a nice clean edge rather than one that looks as though it has been chewed. This makes all the difference to the outline when finished.

The second half of the book deals with the making of a variety of cushions and these will probably spark off some of your own ideas, particularly with different types of fabric and colour combinations.

Whatever you decide to make, I am sure you will find the subject interesting and absorbing and I wish you 'more power to your elbow'.

D.A.G.

1 Loose Cover for a Removable Dining Seat

Estimating

Estimating the amount of cover for a loose seat is a very simple process. First, push the seat out of the chair so that you can take all the measurements. Using a tape measure, take the measurement across the widest part at the front of the seat, from left bottom edge to right bottom edge. Add 12.5 cm. (5 ins.) to each side for turning underneath. Now measure from back to front, adding the turnings as before. (Figure 1)

Two loose seats can usually be made from a width of 122 cm. (48 ins.) fabric by placing them side by side (Figure 2). If, however, the seats are rather larger than average, you may be able to stagger them so that you do not waste a full width on every cut. This is done by measuring the seat at its widest and narrowest points and then adding the turnings. Now see Figure 3 for cutting plan.

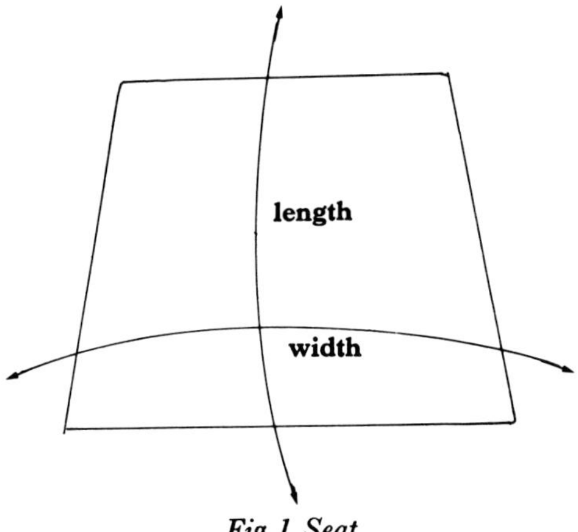

Fig 1 Seat

Another way to save fabric is to place the seats in opposite directions. This may only be done, however, if the fabric has no pile or nap and if there is no definite top and bottom to the pattern (Figure 4). The length taken from front to back, including turnings, will be the amount needed for two seats. You will, of course, have to buy the same amount even if you only need to make one seat as one cannot buy half a width of fabric.

Fitting and Cutting Out

Because the seat may be slightly uneven each side, the fabric should be cut with its right side out. This not only helps to centralize the pattern but is the way it will be lying on the seat when it is finished.

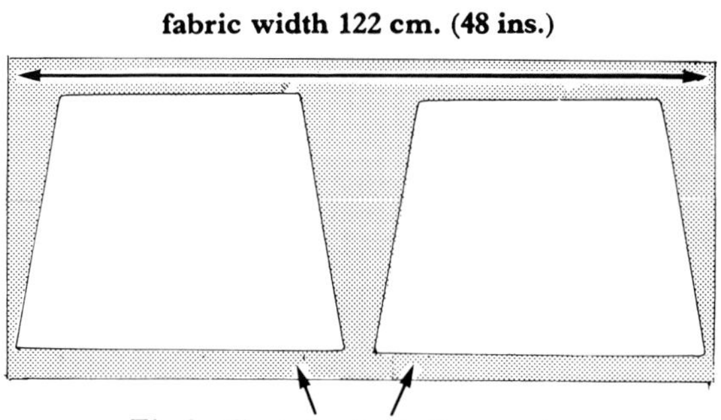

Fig 2 Seat size including turnings

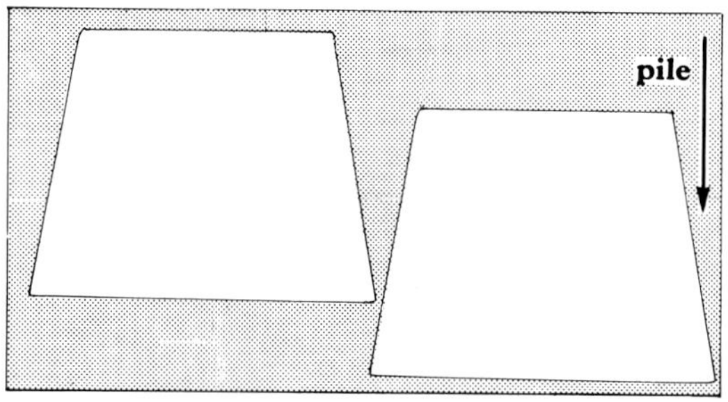

Fig 3 Staggered cutting of seats

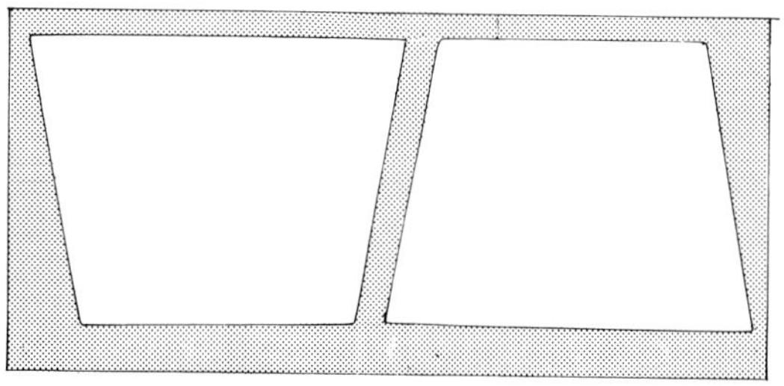

Fig 4 Seats cut in opposite directions

Cut the fabric to size, allowing for the turnings. Now place it on the seat, with the turnings overlapping evenly on all sides, and fix to the seat with a few pins – one each corner will be sufficient (Figure 5).

Turn the seat over so that you are working on the underside and start to pin in the corner darts. (Figure 6)

Pinning the Darts

To pin the darts, hold the fabric as close as you can to the shape of the seat and pin along the outline. Where there is excess fabric over the corners, pin this to form a mitred corner. Now trim off the fabric to leave a 1.25 cm. ($\frac{1}{2}$ in.) turning. Cut small V-shaped notches in the turnings so that these will match up again when the fabric has been unpinned. (Figure 7)

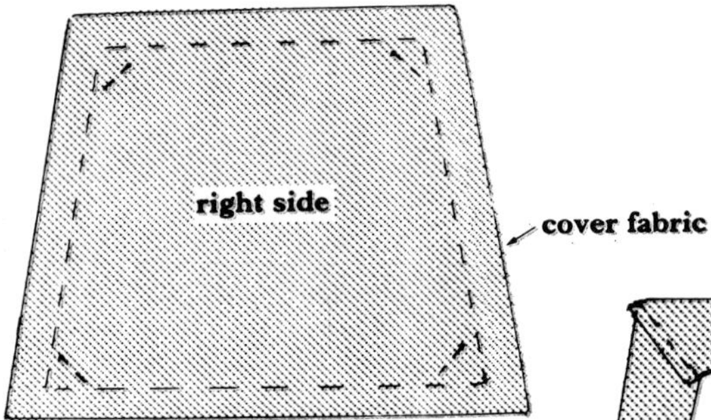

Fig 5

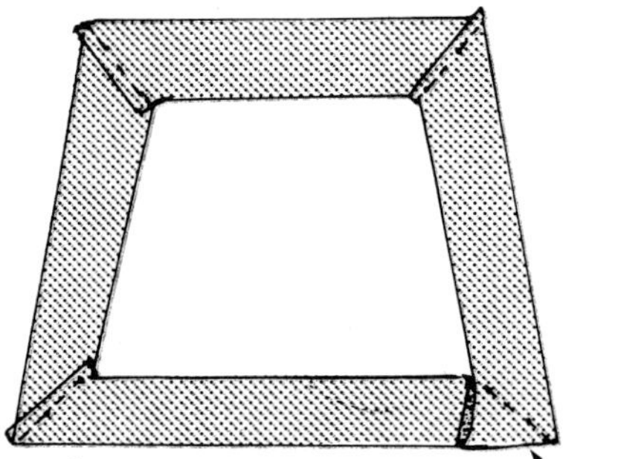

Fig 6

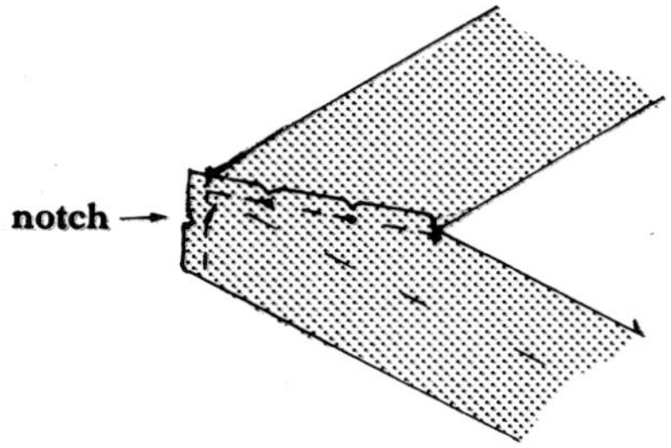

Fig 7

Once all the turnings are trimmed, unpin the turning on the back edge of the seat as far as the corner dart and place a cross pin at this point. You can now take out the top fixing pins and remove the cover from the seat.

Now take all the pins out and reverse the fabric ready for sewing. Re-pin the darts and mitres – but NOT the mitre with the cross pin – matching the notches as you go. Machine down the pin line, starting at the mitred end and finishing with the point of the dart. Reverse stitch at this point to make a firm ending. (Figure 8)

Sewing Up

Start stitching on the open end 1.25 cm. ($\frac{1}{2}$ in.) up from the edge and only stitch the darts up to the turning. (Figure 9)

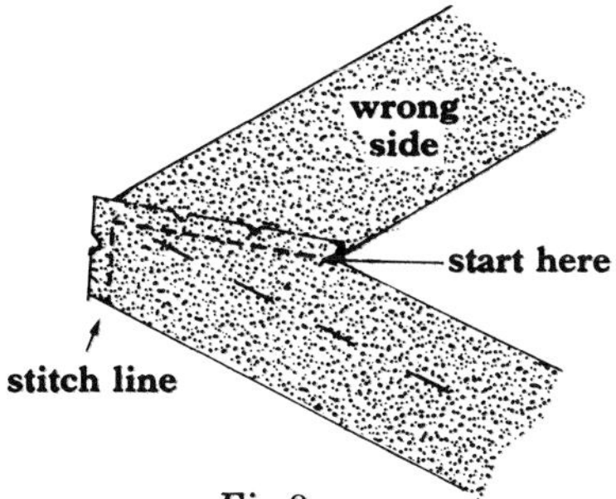

Fig 8

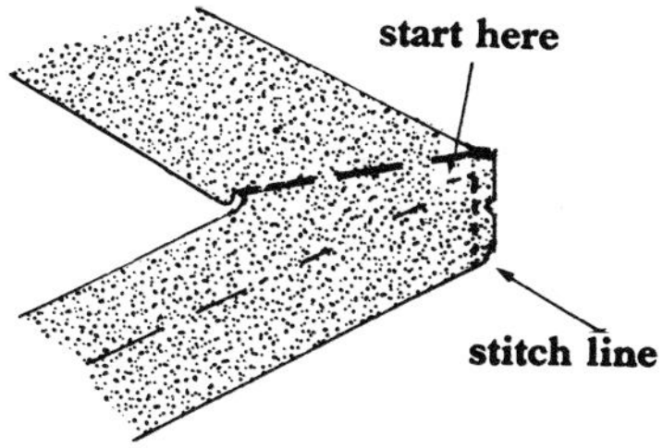

Fig 9

Press all the darts open and then neaten the raw edges, either by machine zig-zag stitch or by oversewing. (Figure 10)

The open mitre must now be taped back to tidy the edges and make an opening. This is done with 1.25 cm. (½ in.) cotton tape, as follows: stitch the tape to the edge of the turning, making a pleat when you reach the corner to enable the fabric to turn back round the sharp point. (Figure 11)

After stitching the first row, turn the tape over to the wrong side of the fabric and stitch down flat; there should now be no tape showing on the right side and only one row of stitching. (Figure 12)

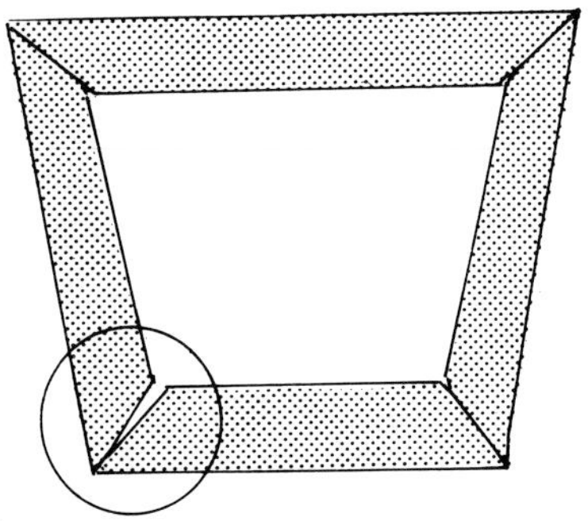

Fig 10

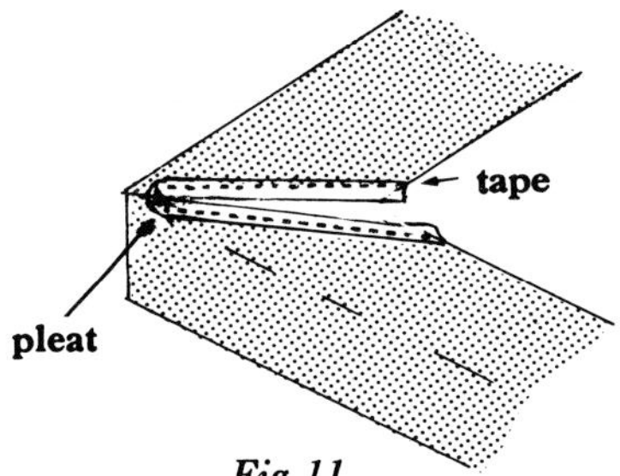

Fig 11

Next, turn the bottom edges up 0.5 cm. ($\frac{1}{4}$ in.) and then 2 cm. ($\frac{3}{4}$ in.); machine this hem all round the seat cover edge, making a firm start and finish.

Cut a length of tape about 45 cm. (18 ins.) longer than the total length of the hem and thread it through the hem using a bodkin or large safety pin. (Figure 13)

Place the cover over the front edges of the seat first so they fit snugly, pull the back corner in place and then, on the open corner, pull the tape that is running through the hems up tight and tie it in a bow. Tuck the ends out of sight, and there you have your loose seat cover.

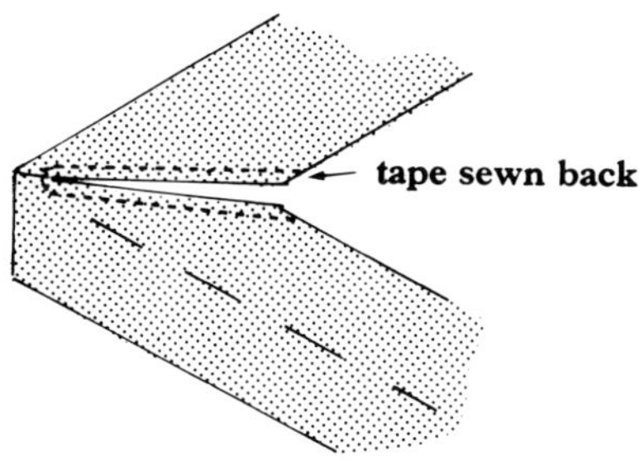

Fig 12

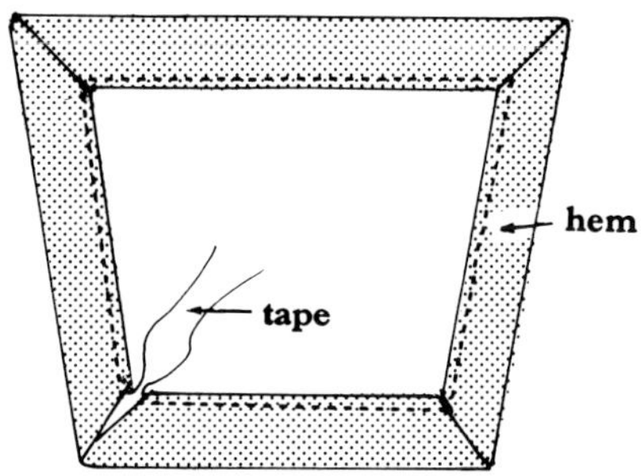

Fig 13

2 *Loose Cover for a Bedroom Chair*

This type of cover can make any small armless chair into a charming bedroom chair. As the legs of such a chair are often ugly the cover includes a frill to give a prettier line.

Estimating

Estimating the amount of fabric for this type of chair is fairly simple; it is a good idea, however, to make a "cut sheet" which will enable you to have all the measurements to hand when you need them. It is assumed that the fabric you have chosen is plain or with a very small repeating pattern. I have given average measurements so do not worry if yours are not quite the same; the main thing is to measure between the correct points.

The arrows denote the length of the fabric and the direction in which it will lie. (Figure 14)

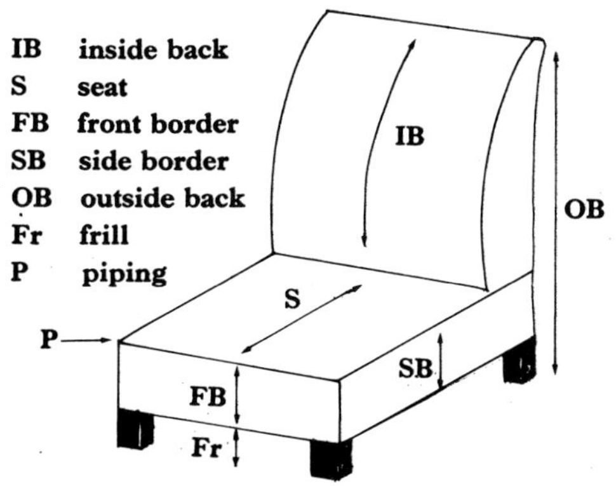

Fig 14 Bedroom chair

The lengths should be measured in the following order:

1 from the top of the Inside Back to the Seat, adding an allowance for the tuck-in and turnings;
2 from the front edge of the Seat to the Inside Back, adding an allowance for tuck-in and turnings;
3 2 Side Borders, 1 Front Border and Outside Back, adding an allowance for turnings only.

To make a "cut sheet", draw out a length of fabric and fit all the pieces into it as economically as you can.

Most furnishing fabric is 122 cm. (48 ins.) wide and so the "cut sheet" is based on this. (Figure 15)

Allowance has been made in the "cut sheet" for the Frill to cover the area around the base twice as well as for the hem and turnings on each piece.

There is a tuck-in on the Seat and Inside Back of 12.5 cm. (5 ins.) on each piece and a turning of 1.5 cm. ($\frac{5}{8}$ in.) at the top, bottom and side of every cut piece.

Having made the "cut sheet" and added all the lengths together, you will now know the total amount of fabric to buy.

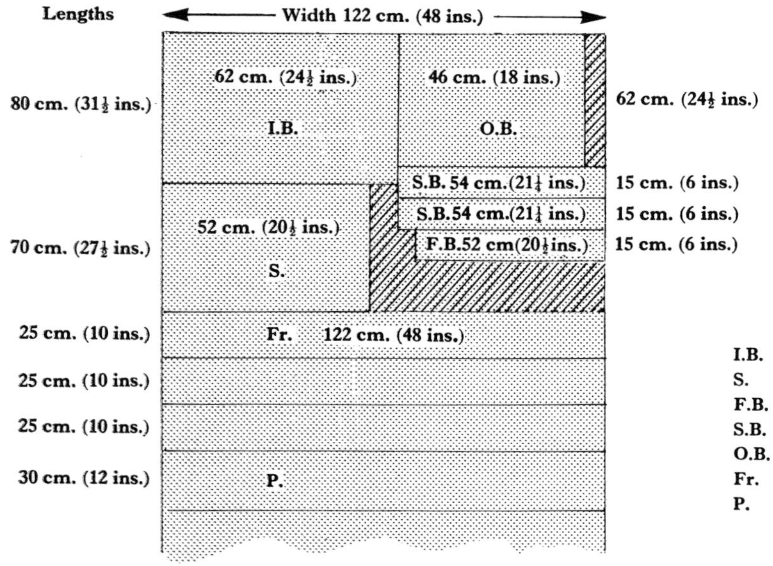

I.B.	80 cm. ($31\frac{1}{2}$ ins.)	62 cm. ($24\frac{1}{2}$ ins.)
S.	70 cm. ($27\frac{1}{2}$ ins.)	52 cm. ($20\frac{1}{2}$ ins.)
F.B.	15 cm. (6 ins.)	52 cm. ($20\frac{1}{2}$ ins.)
S.B.	15 cm. (6 ins.)	54 cm. (two) ($21\frac{1}{4}$ ins.)
O.B.	62 cm. ($24\frac{1}{2}$ ins.)	46 cm. (18 ins.)
Fr.	25 cm. (10 ins.)	122 cm. (three) (48 ins.)
P.	30 cm. (12 ins.)	

Fig 15

Total 2.55 metres ($2\frac{3}{4}$ yards)

Suitable Fabrics

For this type of chair you would not need a very hard-wearing fabric unless, of course, you were to decide to put it in another room where it would receive more use. A cotton, glazed chintz, cotton satin or linen fabric will all make suitable covers. A patterned fabric with a plain piping can look very attractive but takes a little extra fabric.

All the fabrics mentioned are washable, so they are easy to care for. Velvet is *not* suitable for a loose cover as it would crease very badly; also the pile would be inclined to loosen and fall out with the friction on the back of the pile.

To preserve the cover and prevent stains, it is worth spraying the finished cover with a water and dirt repellent spray. These are colourless and, once sprayed on the cover, will last a long time without washing.

Cutting Out

This is the most important part in the making of the cover and should be treated as such. Try to be very accurate in the cutting and in the trimming of the turnings. Cut all the pieces out first and mark each piece on the back. If the fabric has pattern, make sure it is centred and running in line down the Back, Seat and Front Border.

If you mark the top of each piece with a "T" it will save a lot of time later in looking to see the way of the pattern.

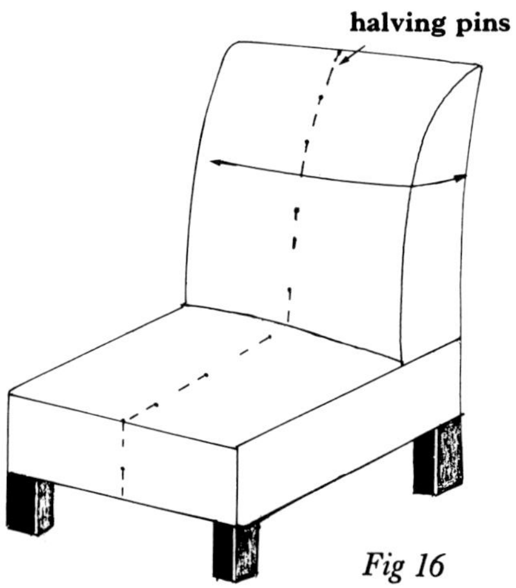

Fig 16

Having cut out all the pieces, you must now "halve the chair". This means measuring the chair across the width and marking the exact centre line with pins. (Figure 16)

Not all chairs can be cut like this; tub chairs or drop-end settees, for instance, would have to be cut "all over", i.e. the fabric could not be halved as the two sides differ on a settee and a tub chair is too rounded to get an accurate halved measurement. The rule, therefore, is only to cut by halving the chair if this is identical on both sides, thus giving a perfect halving. If there is any difference at all in the two sides, then the cover must be cut right over the chair; in this case it is VITAL to cut the fabric with the right side uppermost, otherwise the cover will be in reverse when it comes to fitting it.

The cutting of a cover for a small bedroom chair should not present any such problems, however, even for a beginner.

Cutting the Tuck-in

The only tuck-in pieces on this chair are on the Inside Back and Seat. Having selected them from all your cut-out pieces, start with the Inside Back. Fold it lengthways down the middle, allowing for the turning, and pin to the top edge of the Back. Fix the centre-fold line down the line of pins on the chair and smooth the fabric towards the Outside Back, inserting another pin to secure it. (Figure 17)

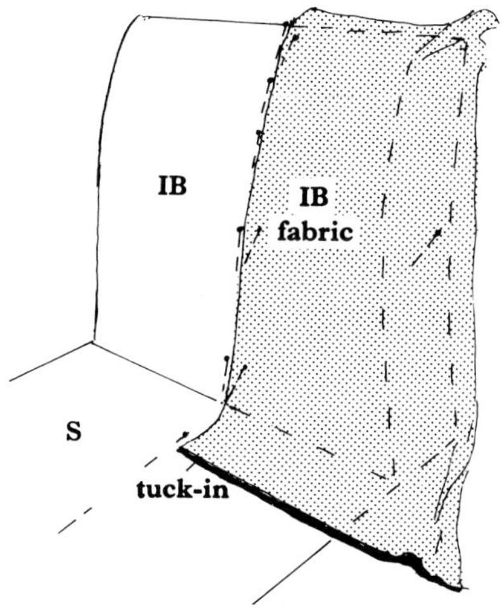

Fig 17

Pin the excess fabric that results at the top corner into a dart and trim back to allow a 1.25 cm. ($\frac{1}{2}$ in.) allowance. (Figures 18 & 19)

When the dart has been trimmed and fitted, smooth the fabric down towards the tuck-in. You will find that the fabric will not tuck-in at the two outer edges because the chair frame stops it; feel with your finger to see how far the frame blocks the fabric and push the fabric in as far as you can in the middle part of the seat. Now mark the point where the frame blocks the free passage of the fabric. Pull the fabric out of the tuck-in and, keeping it smooth, make a slightly slanting cut towards the mark. (Figure 20)

Once this cut has been made you will find that the fabric will move easily to the shape of the chair without dragging.

Smooth the fabric round towards the Outside Back, making another cut *exactly* on the corner where the Inside Back meets the Seat and Side Border. (Figure 21)

Trim the fabric back to 1.25 cm. ($\frac{1}{2}$ in.) for turnings. (Figure 22)

Now take the Seat fabric and fold it in half lengthways, ready to place on the Seat. (Figure 23)

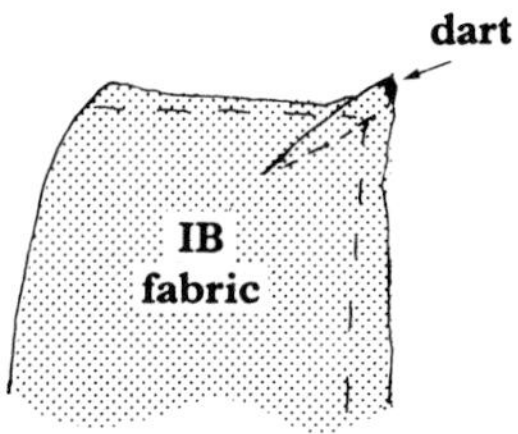

Fig 18

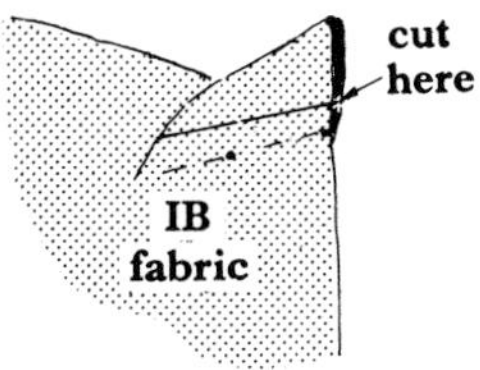

Fig 19

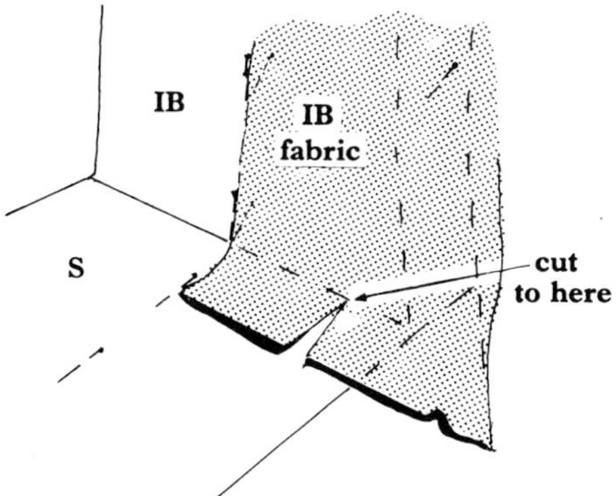

Fig 20

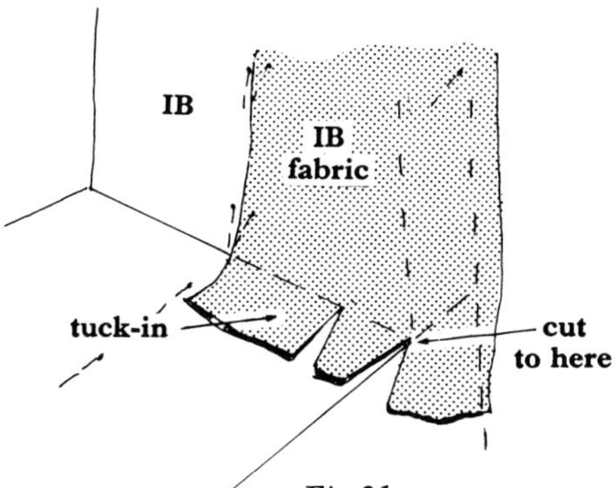

Fig 21

Fitting the Seat

Fit the Seat from the front edge, overlapping the turning. Push the fabric towards the Inside Back until you meet the point of the frame. Cut the fabric at this point so that it lines up with the tuck-in of the Inside Back. Pin the two sections of cover together, leaving the turning allowance. To be on the safe side, notch the cover as you go. If you forget to notch you will find it very difficult to find your way round the cover when you dismantle it to pipe it.

The tuck-in can now be pushed into the gap between the Inside Back and the Seat. This will help to hold the cover in place as well as making sure the tuck-in is not too long and that it fits properly.

Fitting the Borders

You are now ready to fit the other sections, all of which will be the pieces to be piped.

The first piece is the Front Border. This is again folded in half lengthways and pinned to the row of halving pins at the centre of the Front Border. Leave enough overlapping at the top edge for the turning. Keep the fabric running in a horizontal line with the floor and smooth the fabric up to meet the front edge of the Seat.

Pin along the two sections of fabric, joining them together at the exact edge of the chair and following this line along until you reach the corner. Trim the fabric off until only the 1.25 cm. ($\frac{1}{2}$ in.) turning remains, then notch it as before. (Figure 24)

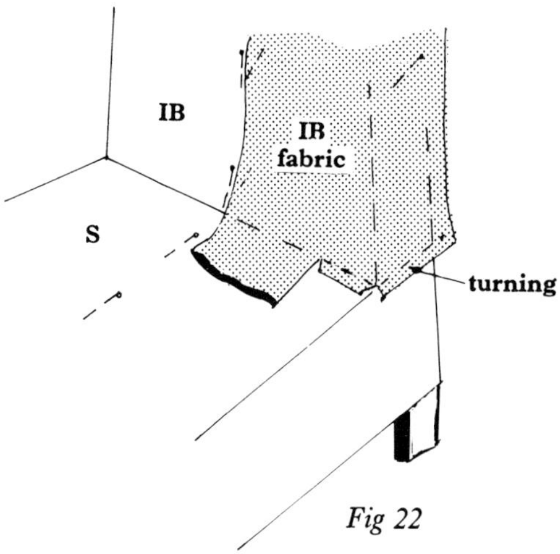

Fig 22

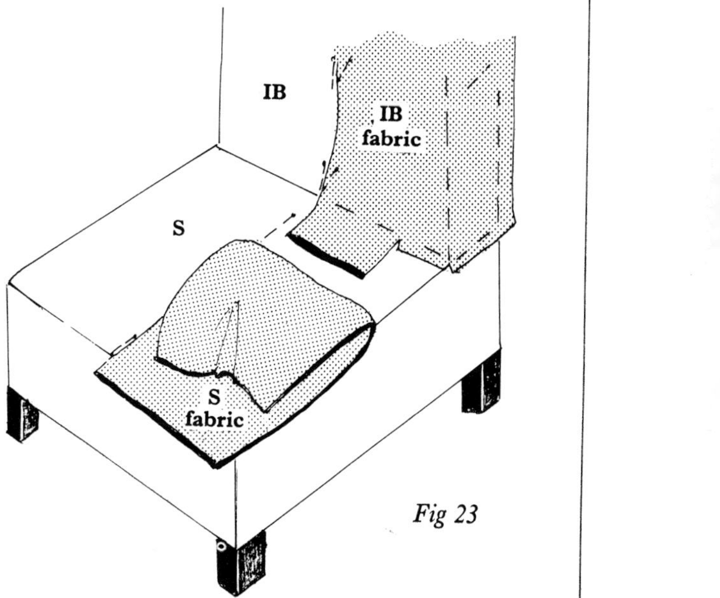

Fig 23

Place the two pieces of Side Border with the wrong sides facing together, so that you have a pair, and put them on the side of the chair with enough overlap at the front for turning. Fix the pieces in place again, lining them up level from the floor.

Pin along the turnings where the Side Border meets the Front Border and then follow the edge of the chair, pinning along the Side Border and Seat. Make a small cut at the juncture where these pieces meet the Inside Back to help you keep the cover properly lined up when you come to sew it. (Figure 25)

Fitting the Outside Back

Having trimmed and notched the sides, the Outside Back can now be fitted in the same way as the other pieces. Fold it in half down the centre length, making sure it lines up with the centre line of pins on the chair.

Pin along the edges to the I.B. and S.B. fabric. (Figure 26) If you do not pin precisely on the outline of the actual chair you will find that the cover will be too big; do remember to feel the edge of the outline as you pin the fabric in place.

Trim off the excess fabric and notch the turnings.

All that now remains to be cut is the level line up from the floor, so that the frill or base finish may be parallel with the floor. To do this, use a wooden or metal rule and measure up from the floor, at intervals of approx. 15 cm. (6 ins.), the depth that you have decided for your frill. On this type of chair, a slightly deeper one is

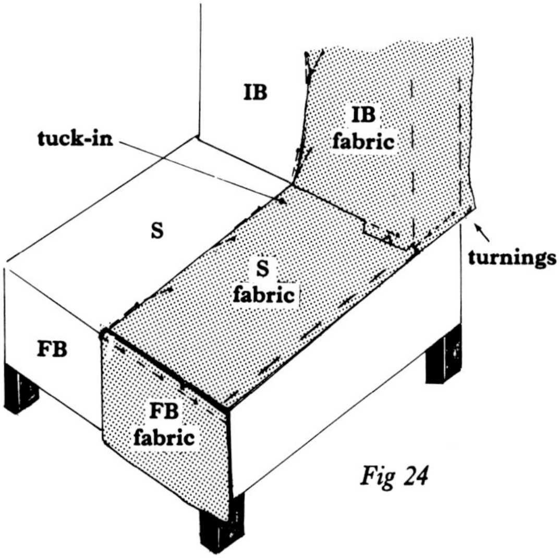

Fig 24

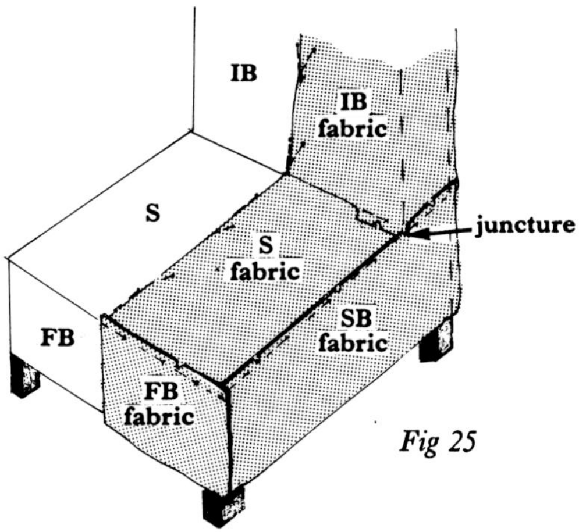

Fig 25

recommended than on an easy chair. For this example, I have chosen a frill with a finished depth of 20 cm. (8 ins.).

Mark a line on the cover 20 cm. (8 ins.) from the floor, using a pencil or a row of pins. This time do not allow extra at the top for turnings because when the turning is made on the finished frill it will bring the frill up 1.25 cm. (½ in.) off the floor; this is necessary to stop the edge of the frill from wearing on the carpet.

On the actual cover, however, you will have to cut 1.25 cm. (½ in.) *below* the marked line so that the turning is not lost on the cover. (Figure 27)

Check that all the turnings are the correct size and that all the notches and junction cuts have been put in.

Now remove the fixing pins from the chair and take the whole cover off carefully, leaving it still pinned together at this stage.

Cut the lengths of frill from the length of fabric and place to one side for later use.

You will now have a length of fabric and a few waste pieces left from which to cut the piping.

Cutting the Piping Strips

It is ideal to cut the piping on the direct cross grain, as it looks much better than straight piping, particularly as loose covers have so many curves. However, if the piping can be cut slightly off the grain it will allow you to cut longer lengths. If you must use straight piping – and I do not recommend it for covers – then

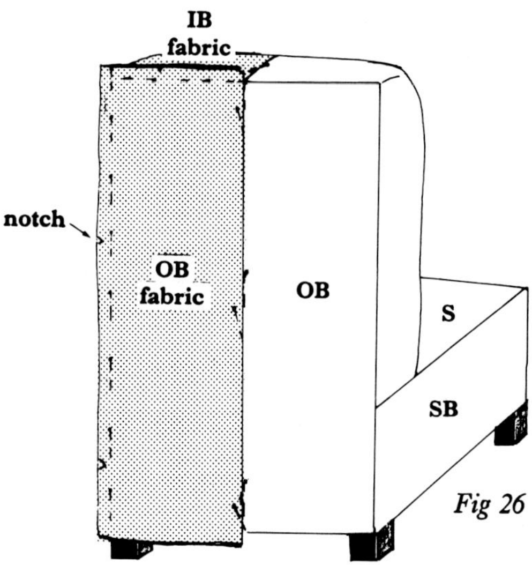

Fig 26

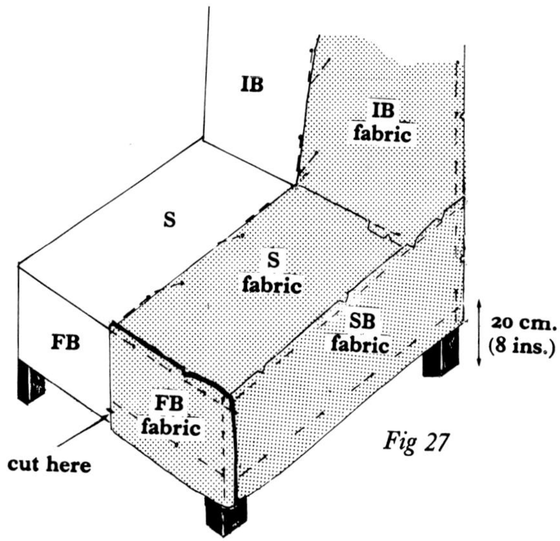

Fig 27

cut across with the weft threads, i.e. from selvedge to selvedge, as they have a greater degree of stretch than the warp.

Fold the piece of fabric across the grain and cut along this fold. (Figure 28) Lay the fabric out flat again and cut off strips of 4 cm. ($1\frac{1}{2}$ ins.) wide (Figure 29). This width will take a medium piping cord; depending on where you buy it, it may be called "00", "no. 4" or just "Medium". If you wish to use a thicker cord then you must increase the width of the piping strips accordingly.

Having cut the piping strips, everything is now ready to start sewing the cover.

Assembling the Cover

The piping – Start the assembling by joining the pieces to make up a length of piping so that it is ready when needed. To do this, lay one piece of piping strip with the right side up and lay a second piece across it with the right side facing down, at right angles to the first piece, so that the join will be at the correct angle.

Sew across this angle (Figure 30) and continue to join all the pieces in a long line. Trim the turnings back to 1.25 cm. ($\frac{1}{2}$ in.) and open them so that they lie flat.

Place the length of piping cord down the centre and fold the piping strip over it. Keeping the edges level and using a zipper foot on the machine, work a line of stitches down the whole length of the piping strip

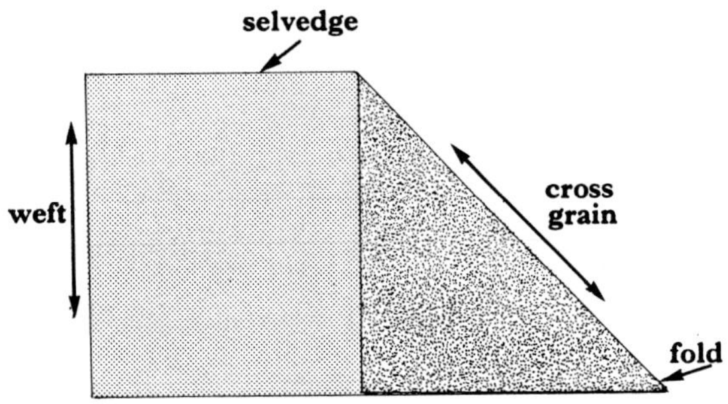

Fig 28

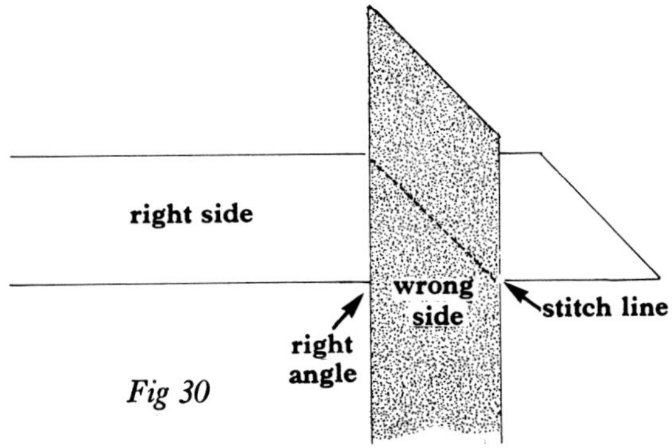

Fig 30

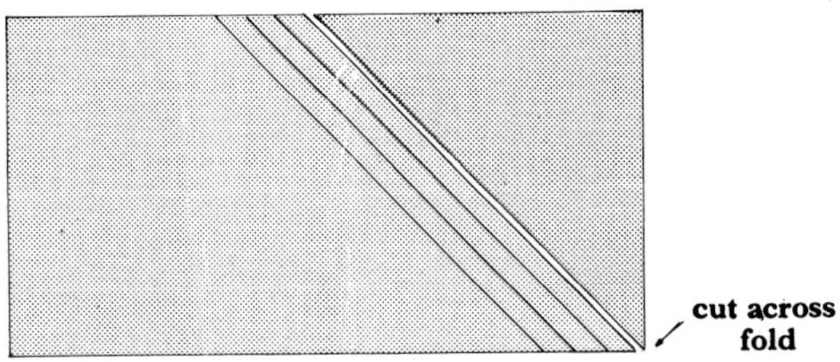

Fig 29

(Figure 31). Do not sew too close to the cord, at this stage, as this line of stitching is only there to hold the cord in place. When you have had more practice, you may find it unnecessary to sew the cord in before inserting the piping but do not omit this stage until you are very practised at piping. It will take you twice as long to unpick a faulty row of stitching than it would have done to work an anchoring row.

Tuck-in assembly – The tuck-in section can now be joined together. First, unpin the outside pieces, i.e. the Outside Back, Side Borders and Front Border, leaving the Inside Back and Seat still pinned to each other.

Unpin these pieces from each other and open them out so that they are single. Mark each dart as it is unpinned so that you will know where to sew it; one dart will be inside out and this should either be marked with chalk or turned so that the dart facing the wrong side of the fabric is facing out, then repin it in position. With the right sides of the fabric facing, pin the Seat and Inside Back together and machine into place. (Figure 32)

If you are used to tacking your work before sewing up, then do so, but pins are really more manoeuvrable when making covers and most people find it better not to tack.

When you have sewn the two sections together, neaten the edges either by using a machined zig-zag stitch or by oversewing. It is a good idea to neaten as you go as it is difficult to tidy up the work after the cover has been assembled.

Fig 31

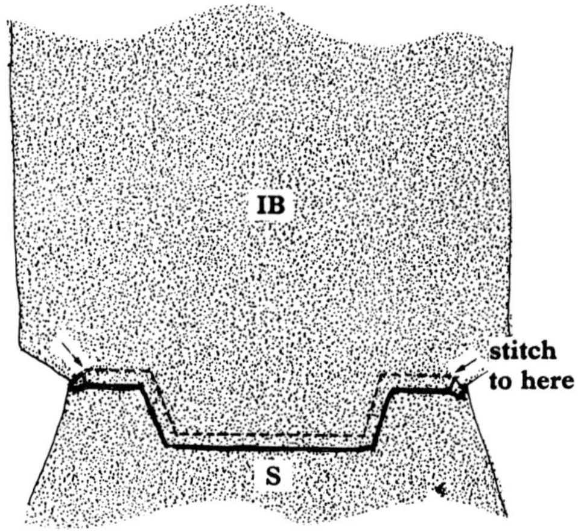

Fig 32

When the Seat and Inside Back have been joined, sew the darts at the top of the Inside Back, starting at the outside edge and tapering to a point; tie the ends of the thread off so that the sewing will remain firm. (Figure 33)

Press the dart flat then place the iron just under the turning so that no impression of the dart is left on the face of the cover. (Figure 34)

Sewing the piping – Now that the tuck-in is complete, put it to one side and prepare to pipe the outside pieces.

First place a length of piping on the two sides of the Front Border. Pin them in place so that the edges of the piping are level with the edge of the fabric. Pull the cord out a fraction at the top and bottom and cut it off, thus enabling the next row of piping to cross this join without having to go over the cord which would make the piping lumpy.

Sew the piping in place, using either a grooved cording foot or a zipper foot, but do not go right up tight to the cord at this stage. (Figure 35)

Pin the Side Borders on either side of the Front Border, matching the notches as you go. Stitch from the piped side so that you can sew inside the stitch line and thus get really close to the cord this time. (Figure 36) Change foot back to the ordinary presser foot on the machine and zig-zag the edges together to neaten.

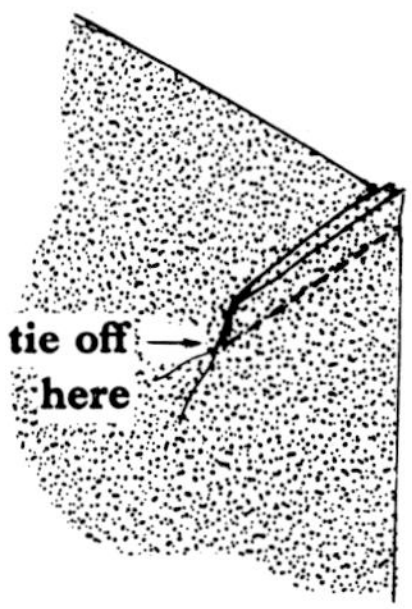

Fig 33

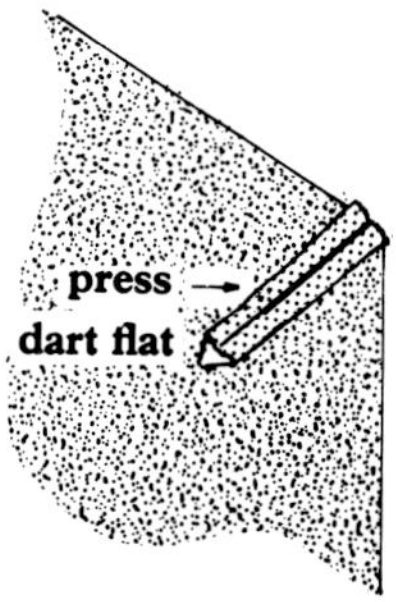

Fig 34

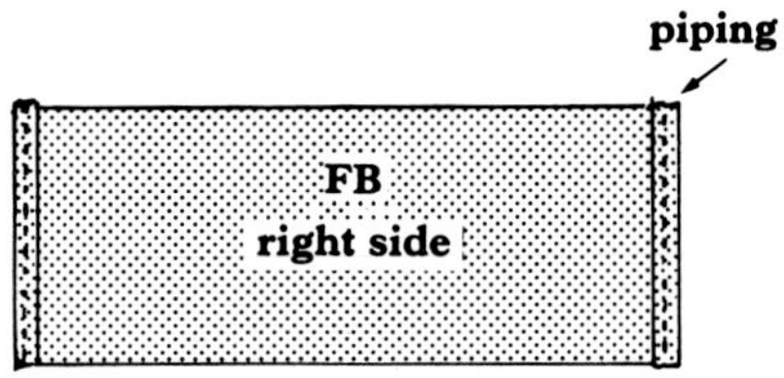

Fig 35

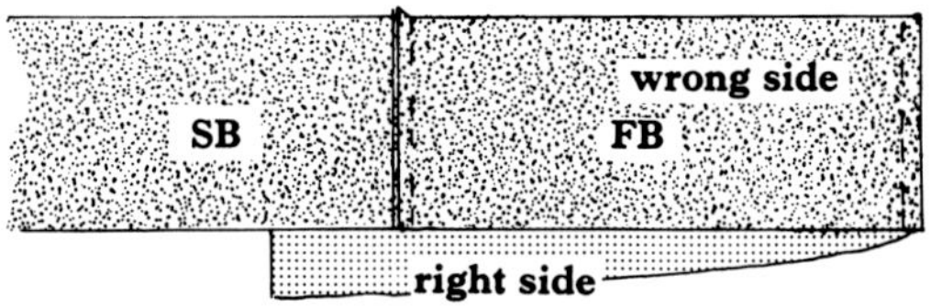

Fig 36

Turn the Border right side out and place the length of piping along the top, starting at the left-hand corner. With the cording or zipper foot machine the piping on, turning the two joins on the Border to face out as a pair as you pass over them.

Continue to pipe all the pieces before assembling them to the tuck-in.

The next piece is the Outside Back. Starting at the lower edge, pin the piping up the side, along the top and, after turning the top corner, pin down the side approximately 7.5 cm. (3 ins.). Leave the length of piping hanging loose but cut it level with the bottom edge. (Figure 37)

This piece of piping transfers to the Inside Back so that the zip, when it has been inserted, is covered from the front view by the piping. Sew the piping in place and then prepare to assemble the rest of the cover.

Sewing the cover – Now that the pieces are all piped, take the 2 Side Borders and the Front Border and pin them to the Inside Back and Seat, taking care to match the notches and the cut at the juncture of the Inside Back, Seat and Border. Machine from the piped side, sewing as close as possible to the cord. Neaten the seam. (Figure 38)

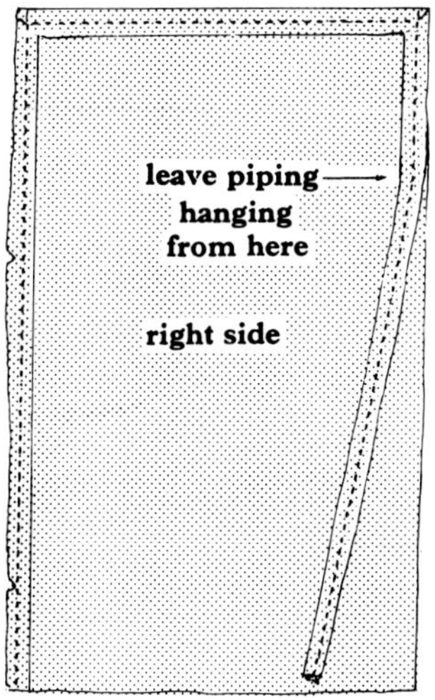

Fig 37

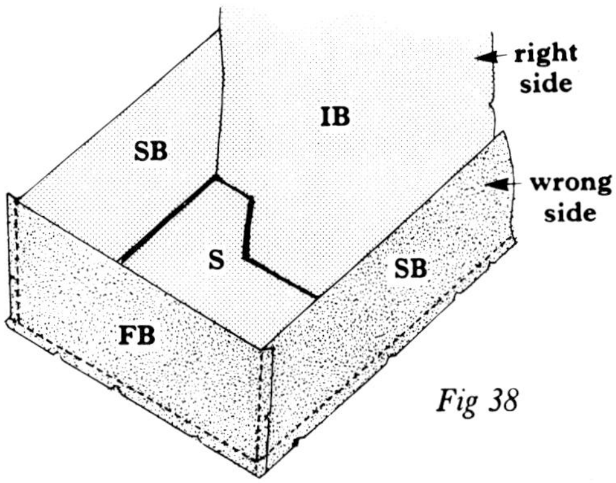

Fig 38

Place the Outside Back in position and pin it to match all the notches. Start machining at the point where the piping was left hanging.

Neaten the edges then place the hanging length of piping on to the Inside Back and Side Border. Pin in place and then machine. (Figures 39 and 40)

Inserting the zip – The cover is now ready to have the zip inserted. Place the zip with the open end at the lower edge and the teeth approximately 1.25 cm. (½ in.) from the edge. There are several methods of sewing in a zip and the following is just one of them, the main object being to sew in the zip as neatly as possible.

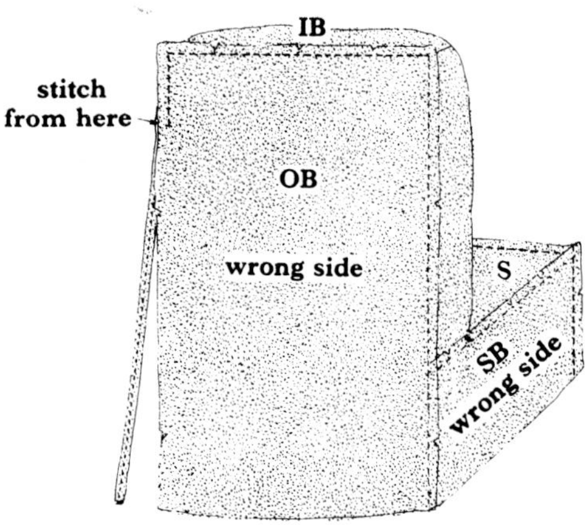

Fig 39

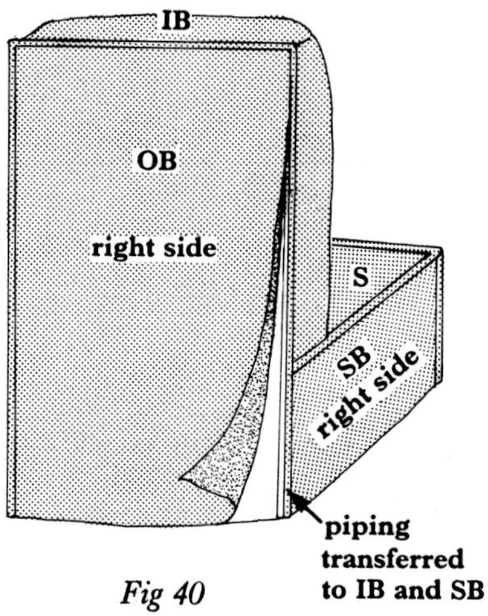

Fig 40

Close the zip and place the right side to the underside of the piped edge, pinning as close to the teeth of the zip as you can. Machine in place down this side of the zip only, stitching in the join where the piping meets the cover. (Figure 41)

Turn the cover the right way out, fold the raw edge in – taking only the amount of turning allowed – and pin in place, covering the teeth (Figure 42). You will now be machining from the right side of the fabric and your top stitching will show on the Outside Back.

Piping the bottom edge – Now pin a length of piping around the entire bottom edge of the cover, starting at the Outside Back. Cut 0.5 cm. ($\frac{1}{4}$ in.) of cord from the end of the piping and turn the raw edges in 1 cm. ($\frac{3}{8}$ in.) to make a neat start where the piping begins.

When you have pinned all round, neaten the end in the same manner as the start. Machine in place. (Figure 43)

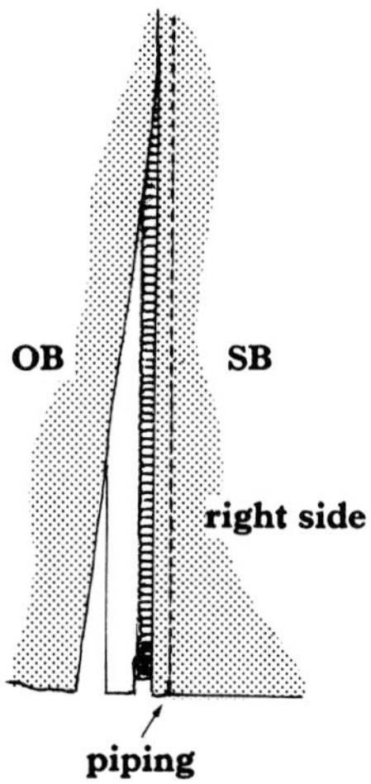

Fig 41

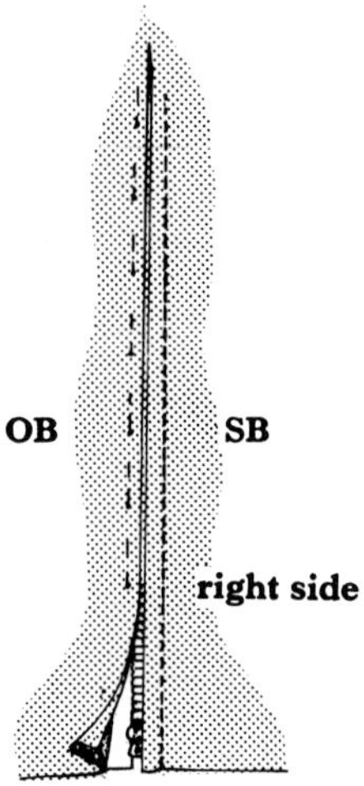

Fig 42

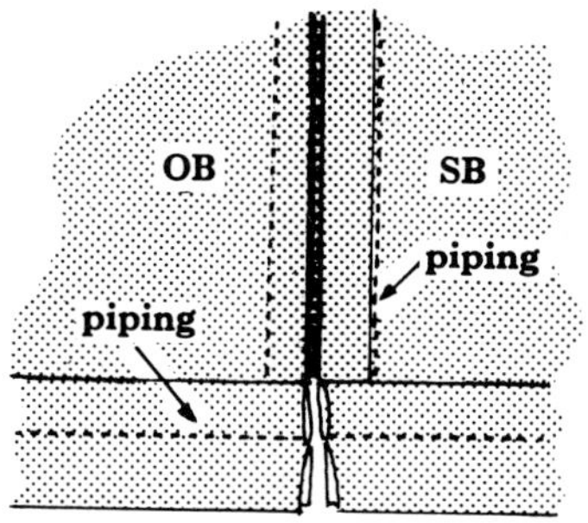

Fig 43

The Frill

To finish the cover, the frill must be made to fit to the lower edge. It can either be lined or unlined. For an unlined frill the following method can be used:

Join all the lengths together in one long line, turn in the side edges 1 cm. ($\frac{3}{8}$ in.) and then turn in a further 2 cm. ($\frac{3}{4}$ in.) and machine. Press open all the joins and then turn the lower edge up 1 cm. ($\frac{3}{8}$ in.) and then a further 2.5 cm. (1 in.). Machine this hem all along the top fold, keeping close to the edge. (Figure 44)

For a lined frill, the following method can be used:

A sateen lining can be used as it is not too heavy and will allow the gathers to fall softly. First of all, cut the three lengths of lining 2 cm. ($\frac{3}{4}$ in.) shorter than the frill. Now join the lengths of lining together and then the lengths of frill. Open out the seams on both pieces and place them with right sides facing together. Pin along the lower edge and machine. (Figure 45)

Turn up the bottom hem 2 cm. ($\frac{3}{4}$ in.) and press along the fold; the lining should be level at the top edge and the fabric will be showing from the wrong side (Figure 46). Turn the side hems in at each end and slip stitch in place.

The frill is now ready to be gathered. From this point, lined and unlined frills are treated in the same way.

Gather the frill along the top edge by using a button thread or 24-gauge thread and sewing a line of running stitch by hand.

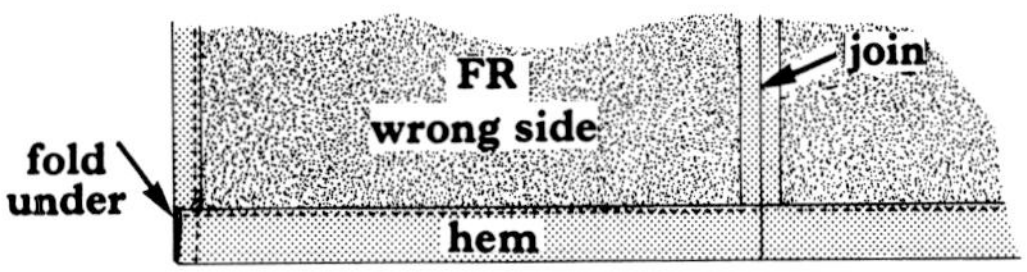

Fig 44

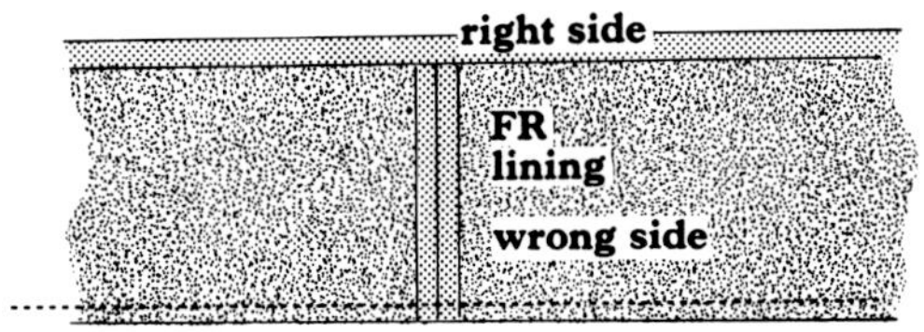

Fig 45

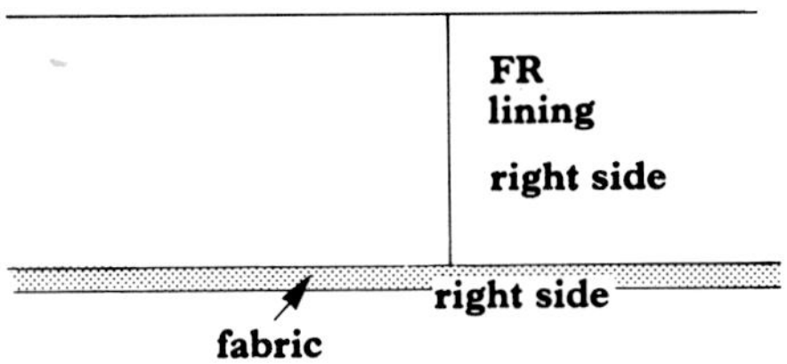

Fig 46

If, however, you have the use of a machine with a zig-zag stitch on it the following method can be used. Using the ordinary presser foot on the machine, turn the stitch to a fairly large zig-zag. Anchor a length of thick thread with a pin to the top edge of the frill approximately 1.25 cm. ($\frac{1}{2}$ in.) from the top. Work in zig-zag stitch over the thick thread, being careful not to catch it.

When the sewing is finished, leave about 5 cm. (2 ins.) of the thread hanging from the end, ready to pull and gather up the frill. (Figure 47)

Now measure half-way along the top edge of the frill and mark with a pin. Then divide again into two and mark so that you now have one half and two quarter marks. (Figure 48)

Measure around the base of the chair and mark the halves and quarters in the same way.

Lay the chair cover on to the frill, right sides facing, and match up the pins. Now pull the thick thread up so that it gathers the frill. Even the gathers out between each quarter mark (Figure 49) and pin the chair cover to the frill all the way round. Leave about 2.5 cm. (1 in.), both at the beginning and the end so that these pieces can later be folded back to make the ends tidy.

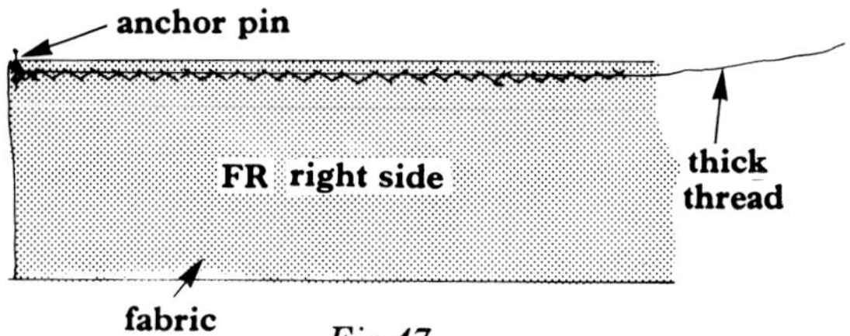

Fig 47

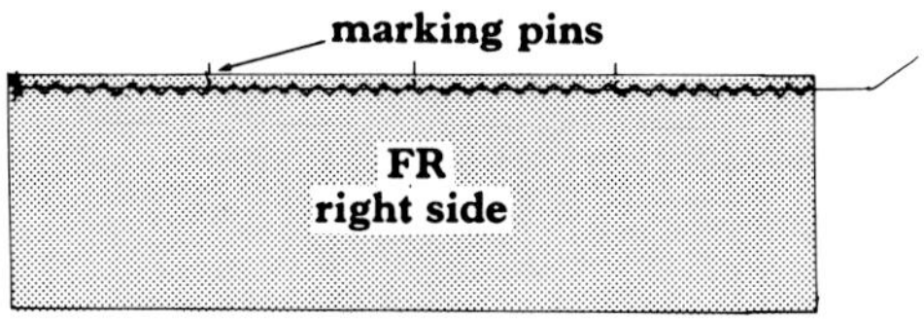

Fig 48

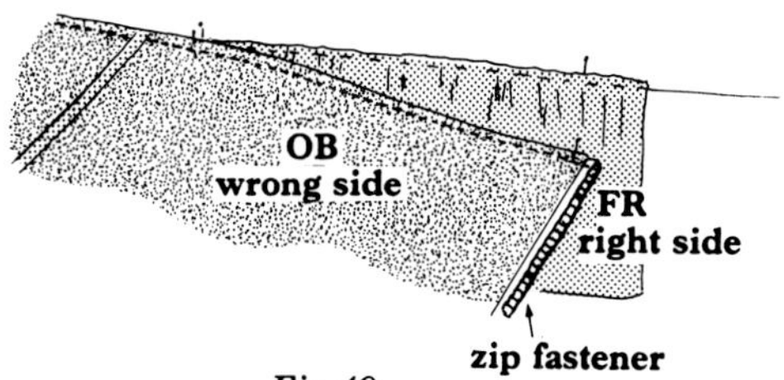

Fig 49

Machine the frill to the cover, keeping the stitching up tight to the piping cord. Fold back the frill at the ends and machine into place. (Figure 50)

Neaten the edges and press the finished cover. (Figure 51)

The Kick-pleated Base

This is an alternative to the frilled base. Measure across the Front Border and add 20 cm. (8 ins.). Measure the two Side Borders and add 20 cm. (8 ins.) and then measure across the Outside Back adding another 20 cm. (8 ins.). Join the four lengths, making sure you have them in the correct order to apply to the cover; this will be:

Side Border, Front Border, Side Border, Outside Back. If you want to have the chair opening on the other side, then reverse this order. (Figure 52)

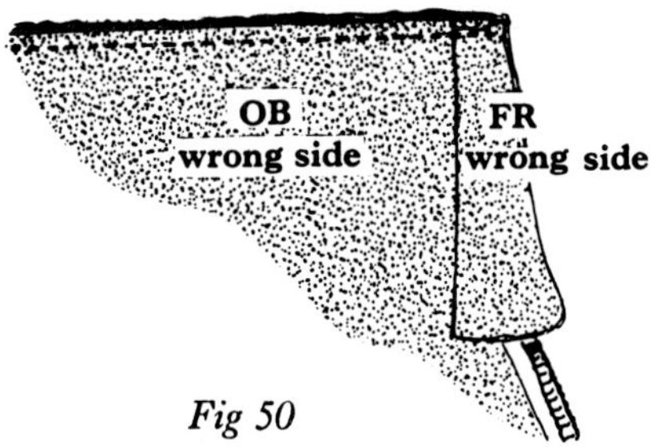

Fig 50

Fig 51 Bedroom chair with a frilled base

Start and stop with half a pleat, folding back the end as described in the instructions for the frill (Figure 50). At each corner fold the excess fabric to form a pleat, keeping the join to one side so that it will not show if the pleat opens.

Apply the kick pleat to the cover keeping close to the cord and making sure the pleat meets at each corner. Press the cover and make a nice sharp crease in each pleat.

Fitting the Cover

The sequence for fitting the finished cover on to the chair is:

1 slip the Back over the back of the chair;
2 place the Front Border into position;
3 tuck in the Seat and Inside Back;
4 fasten the zip;
5 turn the piping so that it all faces in one direction; this will make the turnings lie flat and give a better appearance to the whole chair. (Figure 53)

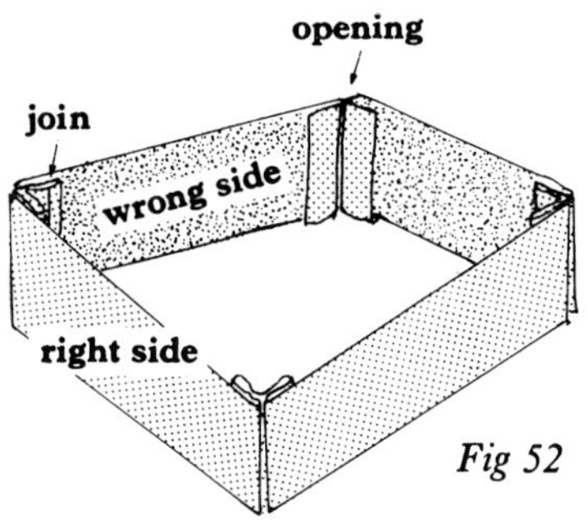

Fig 52

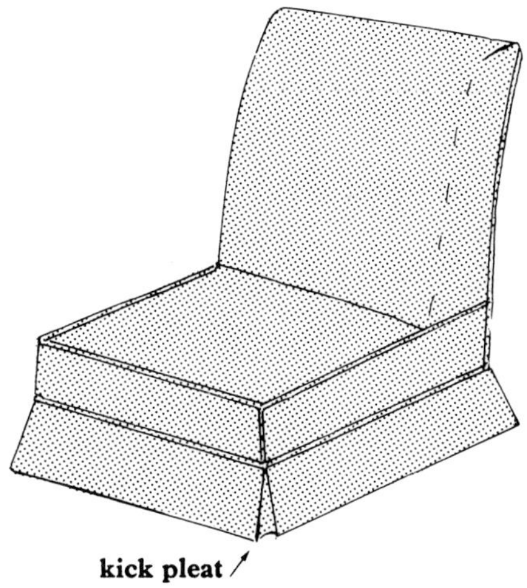

Fig 53 Bedroom chair with a kick-pleated base

3 *Loose Cover for a Wing Chair*

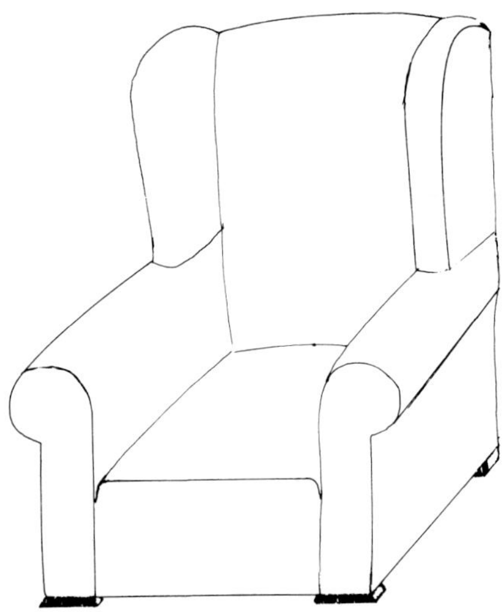

Fig 54

Many of the processes used in the previous chapter are used on the wing chair, so instead of repeating them I will refer back when such points arise.

A wing chair is, of course, much more complicated than a small bedroom chair. However, if you have learned to pipe, to insert a zip and are able to fit a chair snugly, then there is no reason why you should not make a success of this more difficult task.

Figure 54 shows a basic wing chair; there are variations, of course, but this type includes as many processes as possible to enable you to cope with any difficulty.

Halving the Chair

This must be done very accurately as all the fitting depends on the halving being correct. Measure across the width of the chair at intervals. The most important points are at the bottom edge of the Outside Back, the Front Border, the top of the Inside and Outside Back and the front edge of the Seat.

There are two points on the Inside Back that must be marked; these are between the base of the wings and at the base of the Back where it meets the Seat. The reason for this is that the frame has to be allowed for and so the fabric must be cut to cover these areas.

An explanation of how to make a "cut sheet" has already been given and this type of chair will need to be measured and estimated in exactly the same way. The style of this cover is a tie-under style which means you will have to allow an extra 15 cm. (6 ins.) on the lengths of the Outside Back, Outside Arms, and Front Border. This extra will pull underneath the chair, when the cover is finished, thus holding it secure and giving a tailored finish.

On the *length* of the Inside Back and the Seat an extra 15 cm. (6 ins.) must be added for tuck-ins. And on the *width* of the Inside Back and Seat 15 cm. (6 ins.) must be added to *each* side. The Inside Arms require an additional 15 cm. (6 ins.) tuck-in on both the width and the length. The Inside Wings have 15 cm. (6 ins.) added to their width. The list of pieces to cut is shown in Figure 55.

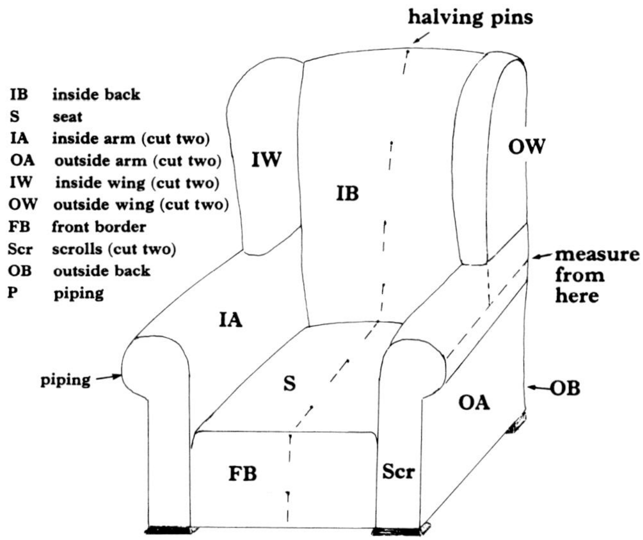

Fig 55

Measure the chair carefully and make a "cut sheet", fitting all the pieces in so that you will be able to use the "cut sheet" both to estimate the amount of fabric required and as a check list to make sure that you have cut all the pieces out. (Figure 55)

Cutting and Fitting

Start with all the inside pieces as these are used to make up the tuck-in. Fold the Inside Back down the middle of its length and pin to the line of pins down the back of the chair. Leave enough to overlap at the top edge for turnings.

Fit the Seat in the same way starting at the front edge and again leaving enough for turnings.

Pin the tuck-in section together, taking in the 1.25 cm. (½ in.) turnings, then trim and notch.

Place the two Inside Arms together, pairing them so that the wrong sides are facing. Fix the front of the arm so that the turning is overlapping the chair. The Inside Arm on this type of chair joins on the outer edge or sight line which, looking from the front, is half-way down the bulbous part of the arm. (Figure 56)

Keeping the fabric grain level with the floor line, pin with a few pins to hold it in place. Smooth the fabric towards the Inside Back; when it comes in contact with the Inside Wing, you will find it needs to be cut to allow it free passage to get to the tuck-in. (Figure 57)

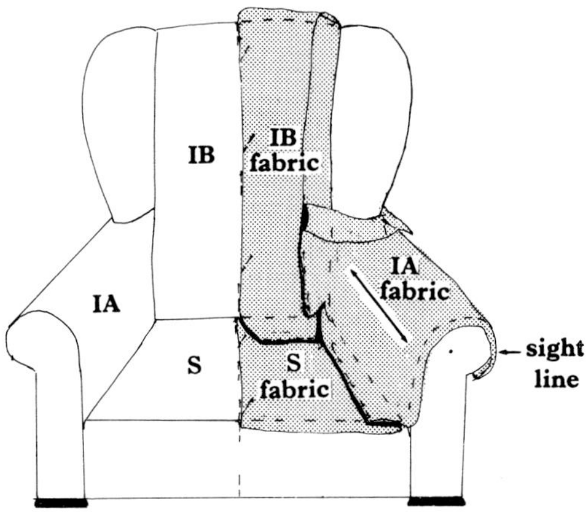

Fig 56

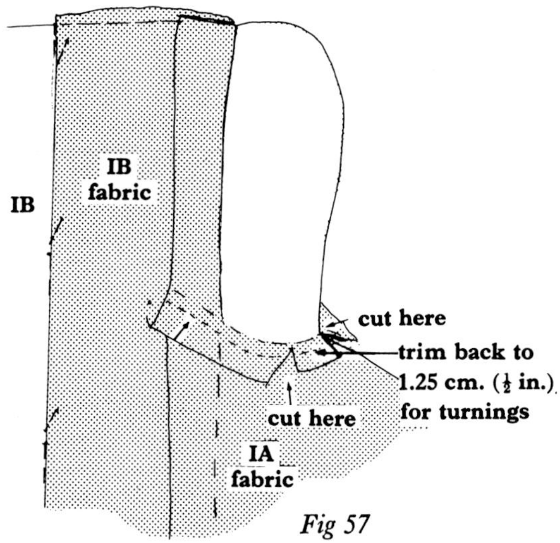

Fig 57

Cut the fabric round the Wing and trim back so that you have a 1.25 cm. ($\frac{1}{2}$ in.) turning; where the Arm tuck-in meets the Inside Back tuck-in, pin together, trim and notch. (Figure 58)

The next parts to cut are the Inside Wings; again, make sure they are paired, with wrong sides facing. Keep the fabric upright, fix with a few pins to hold in place and then make identical cuts at the base of the Wing to match the Inside Arm. Pin the two together, trim and notch. (Figure 59)

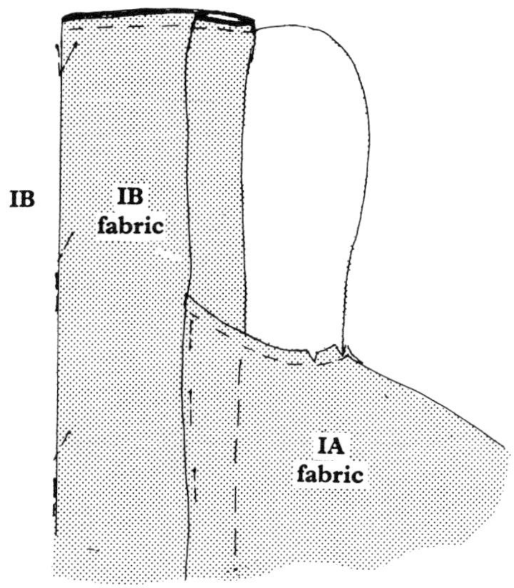

Fig 58

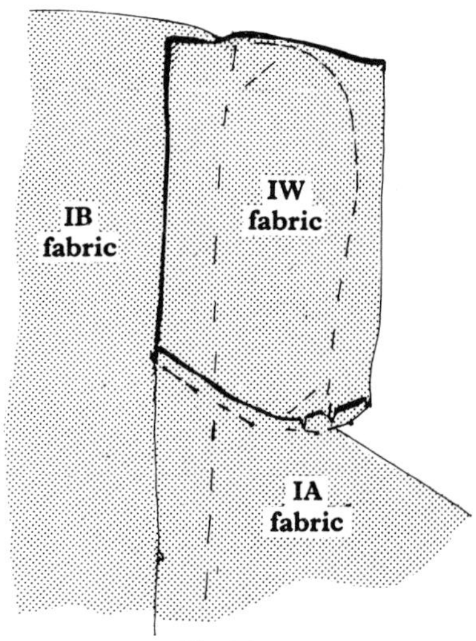

Fig 59

Push in the tuck-in at the top of the Inside Back as far as it will go; the frame will obstruct you about 15 cm. (6 ins.) down from the top and this must be cut round to allow the cover to fit well here. (Figures 60 & 61)

The Wing will have some surplus fabric where it turns round to follow the contour at the top of the wing. Two darts are usually sufficient to take in this excess fabric.

Pin the darts in so that they take up the fullness, then trim the fabric back to 1.25 cm. ($\frac{1}{2}$ in.). (Figure 62)

Where the Seat and Inside Arm meet, pin these two pieces of tuck-in together, trim and notch. The tuck-in is now complete.

The outside pieces are now added to the cover; these pieces are much easier to fit as they follow the basic outline of the chair.

The first pieces to add are the Outside Arms; pair these up with wrong sides facing together, overlap the turning at the front edge and leave the 15 cm. (6 ins.) extra to fall below the frame line. Fix with a few pins, one under the edge of the Scroll and one at the Outside Back, placing them in line so that the fabric will dip in. Keep the fabric horizontal with the floor. (Figure 63)

Pin and trim along the sight line and notch the turnings.

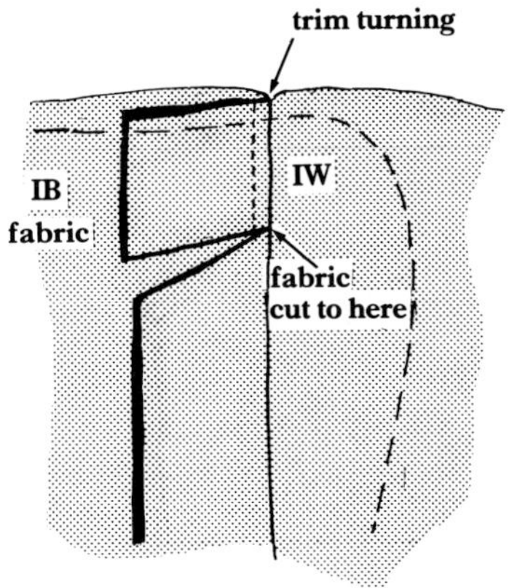

Fig 60

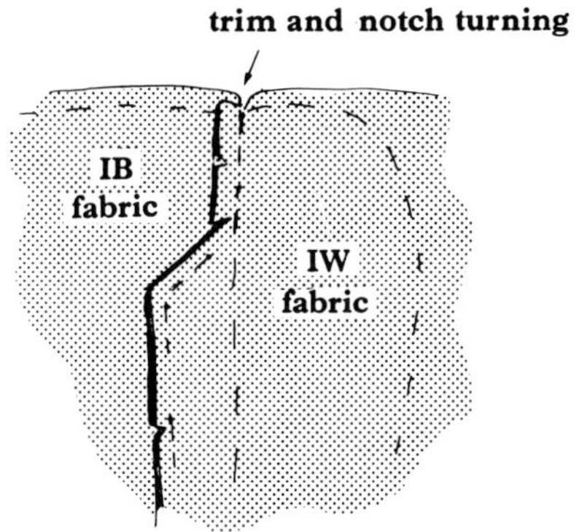

Fig 61

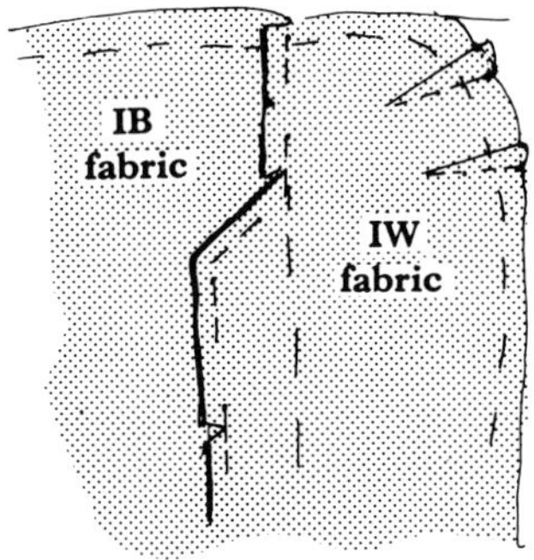

Fig 62

The Outside Wing is fitted next. Keeping the fabric upright, fix with a few pins to hold its position. Following the outline of the Wing, pin the fabric where it joins the Inside Wing and the Inside and Outside Arms, taking special care to pin right into the corners. Trim back and notch. (Figure 64)

Push the tuck-in down at the front of the Seat as far as it will go. Then, folding the Front Border down its length, pin it around the front edge of the chair, following the fabric where it is tucked in. Trim, leaving the turning, and notch. Make a cut where the tuck-in finishes on the Front Border.

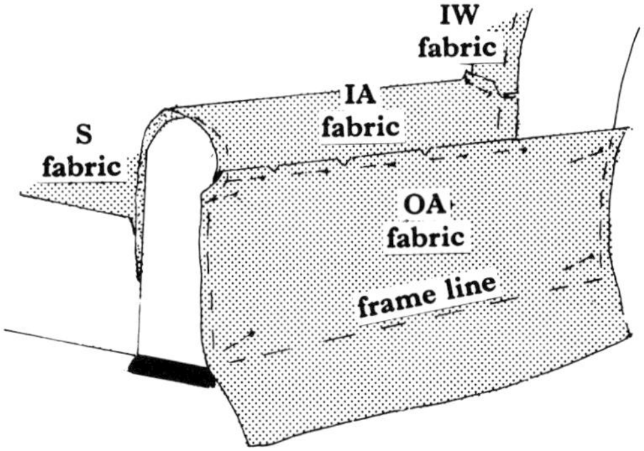

Fig 63

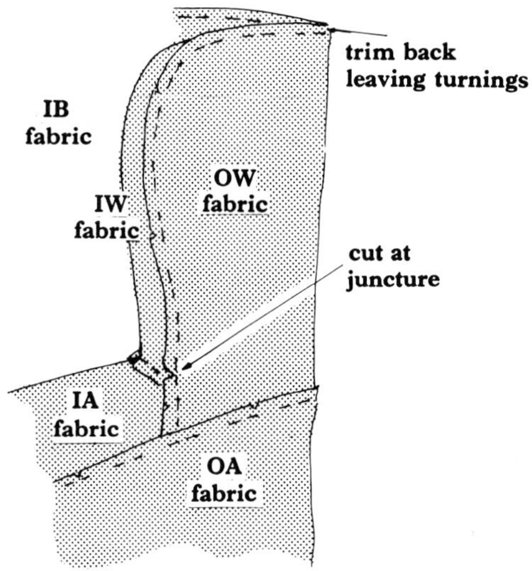

Fig 64

To link up the Front Border and Arms the Scrolls are now fitted. They must be paired, with wrong sides facing. Follow the outline of the Scroll on the chair and pin to ensure a good line. Join the Scrolls to the Front Border, Inside Arm and Outside Arm. Trim back to 1.25 cm. ($\frac{1}{2}$ in.) and notch. (Figure 65)

The last section to fit is the Outside Back. Again the length of fabric must be folded down the middle and pinned to hold it level. Starting at the sides, pin the outline of the chair up towards the top, then start again in the middle of the top of the Back and smooth the excess fabric out to the corners. Pin, trim back to a 1.25 cm. ($\frac{1}{2}$ in.) turning and notch. (Figure 66)

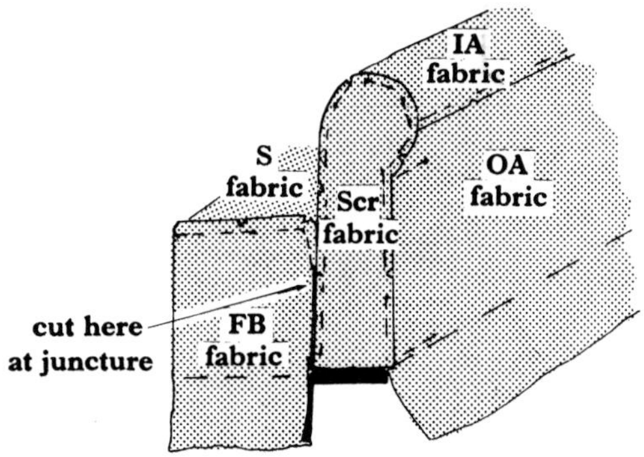

Fig 65

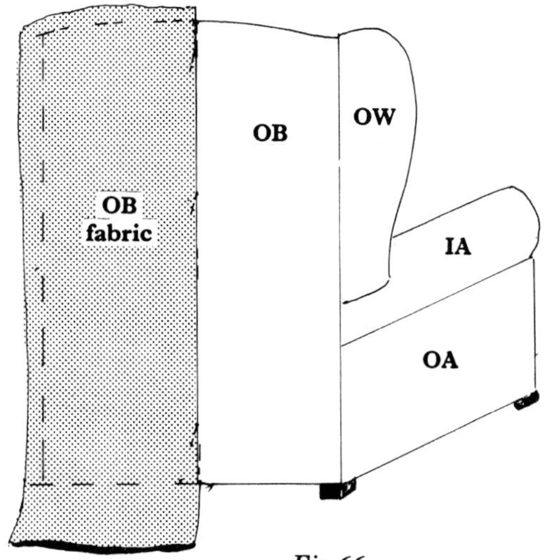

Fig 66

Turn the chair up so that you can get to the underside and, following the diagram, cut around the legs so that the fabric will lie correctly to make a tailored (tie-under) style cover. (Figure 67)

Take out all the pins that are fixing the fabric to the chair and remove the cover in one piece. You are now ready to sew.

Assembling the Cover

On this particular cover, we have to pipe a few pieces before we can assemble the tuck-in. The area we pipe is at the top of the Inside Back where it joins the Wings and at the top of the Inside Arm where it joins the Wings.

Piping the tuck-ins – Unpin all the outside pieces, as these will be piped later.

The tuck-in area consists of the Inside Back, Seat, Inside Arms and Inside Wings. Using the zipper foot, pipe the Inside Back as shown in Figure 68.

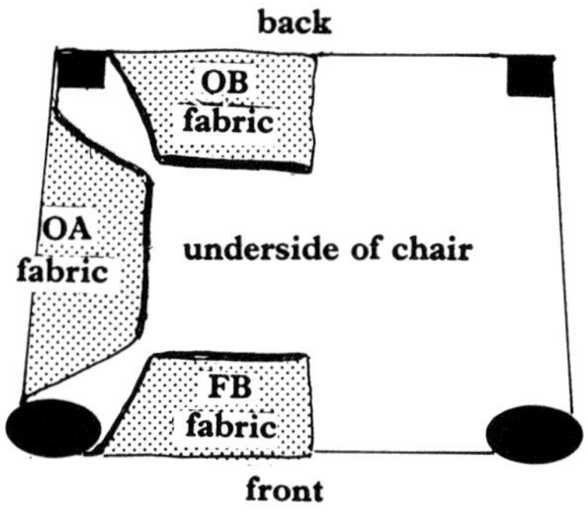

Fig 67

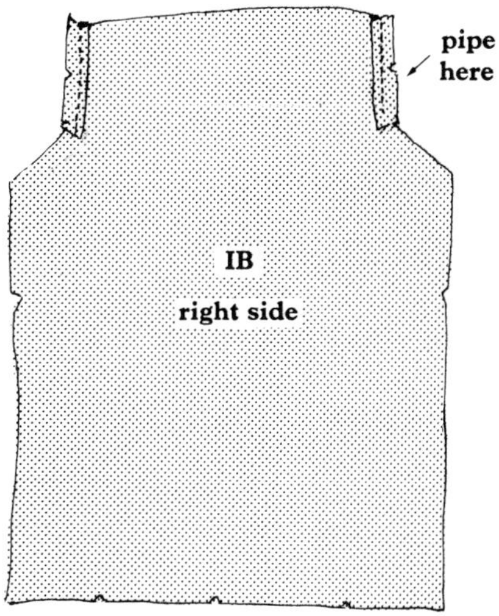

Fig 68

Now pipe the Inside Arm. (Figure 69)

Assembling the tuck-ins – Join the Inside Wing to the Inside Arm, overlapping the piping past the cut. Sew to cut only. Repeat this for the other Wing.

Join the Wing and the Inside Arm to the Inside Back, on both sides. You can now replace the ordinary pressure foot and neaten the edges of the seams.

Sew the darts on the Inside Wing (page 34) and press open. Pin the Seat to the Inside Back and machine across. Neaten the edges.

Pin the Seat to the base of the Inside Arms, starting at the front edge. Machine along this seam and neaten the edges (Figure 70). The tuck-in is now complete and you are ready to pipe the outside pieces.

Piping the outside pieces – In Figures 71–74 I have shown where to start and stop each piece of piping. Check list:

1. On the Outside Arms, pipe straight across the tops.
2. On the Scrolls, pipe from the bottom edge right round to bottom edge, snipping the piping to allow it to go round the curves.

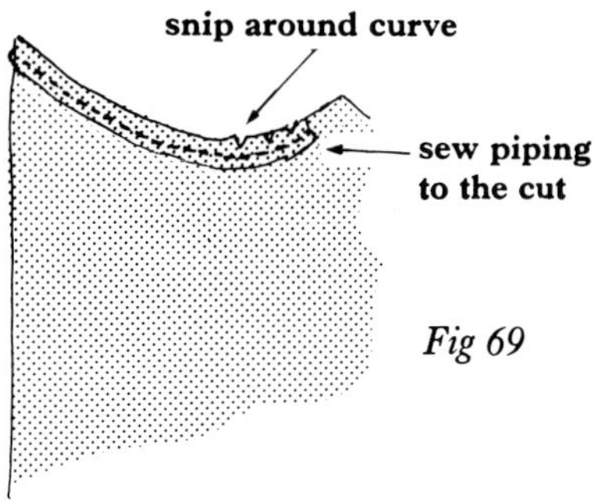

Fig 69

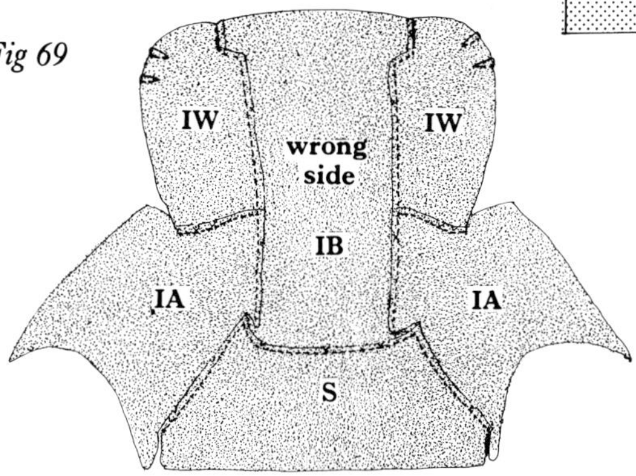

Fig 70

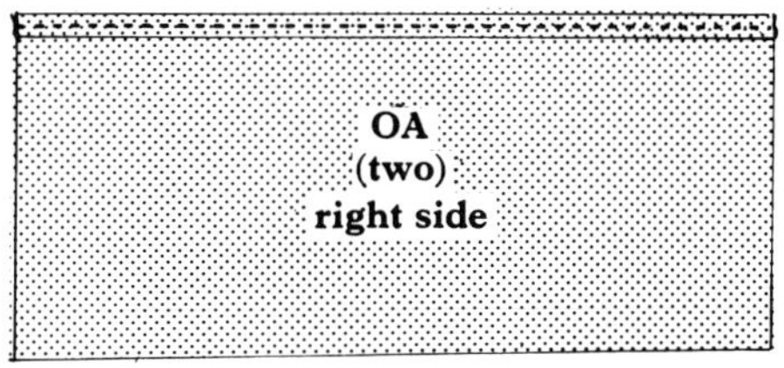

Fig 71

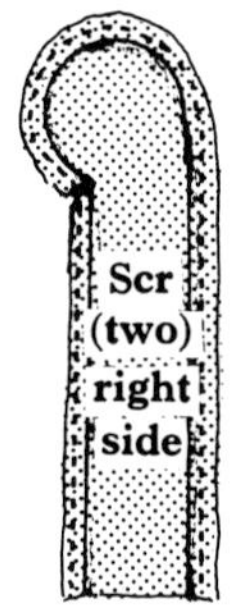

Fig 72

3 On the Front Border piping starts just below the cut; start the machining right on the cut and finish in the same way.

4 The Outside Back is piped down both sides. One is piped all the way down but on the other side the piping is stitched down to about 15 cm. (6 ins.) from the top edge and then left hanging. (See page 23)

5 The Outside Wings are then attached to the Outside Back and a length of piping machined from the bottom edge of the Wing right round, across the top of the Back and round to the bottom of the other Outside Wing.

Assembling the outside pieces – Having completed the piping, join each piece so that the piping overlaps neatly at the junctures without dragging. The first pieces to attach are the Outside Arms; match the notches up to the Inside Arms, pin, machine and neaten as you go. (Figure 75)

Fig 73

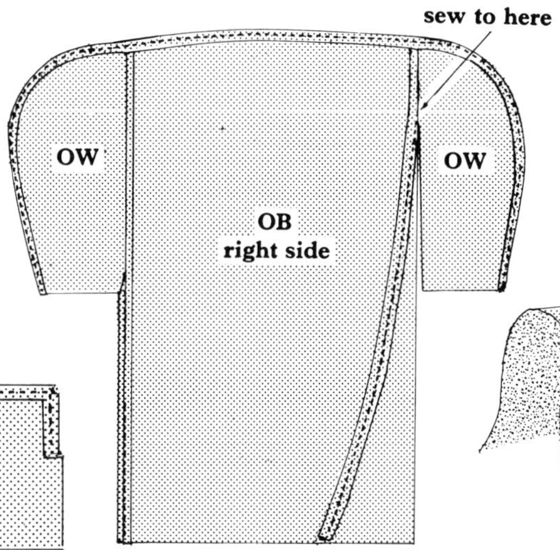

Fig 74

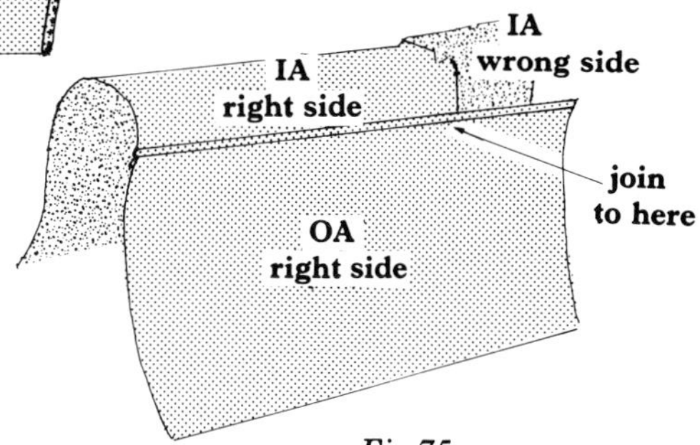

Fig 75

Next join the Front Border to the Seat, starting at the small cut and finishing in the same manner. (Figure 76)

The Scrolls are pinned in place next; when they meet the Front Border you may have a little difficulty as the piping must cross over on to the lower part of the Front Border and you should make sure that the fabric is all caught in otherwise you may find a hole has been left in it. (Figures 77 & 78)

Before you complete the Outside Back, finish sewing the piping on the Outside Arm to join up to the base of the Outside Wings. Machine into position and then neaten. (Figures 79 & 80)

Having finished the front, the Outside Back and Wings can be pinned in next. Start at the lower edge of the Outside Wing and join it to the Inside Wing; continue right round the Wings, across the Outside Back and down the other Wing. Machine and neaten seams.

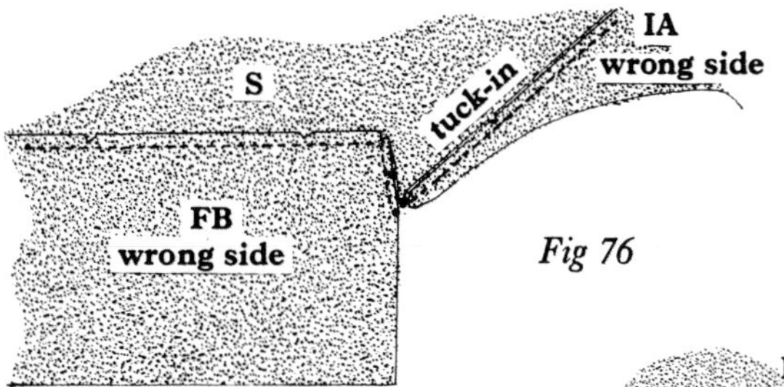

Fig 76

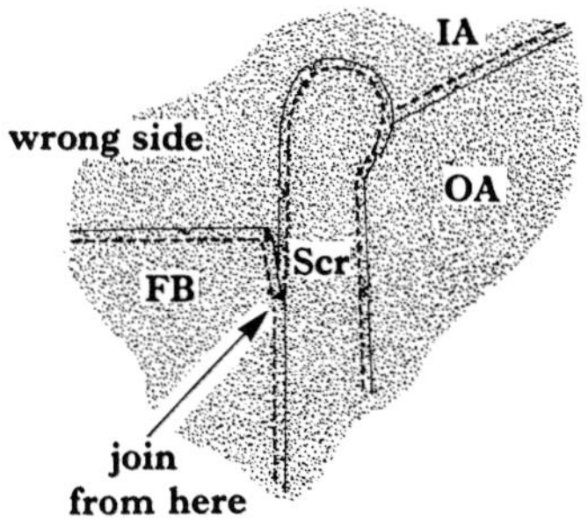

Fig 77

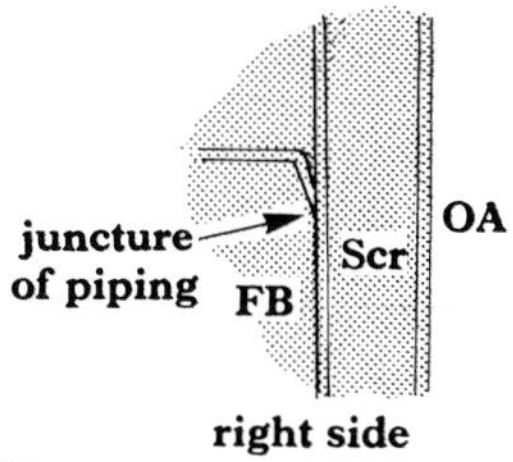

Fig 78

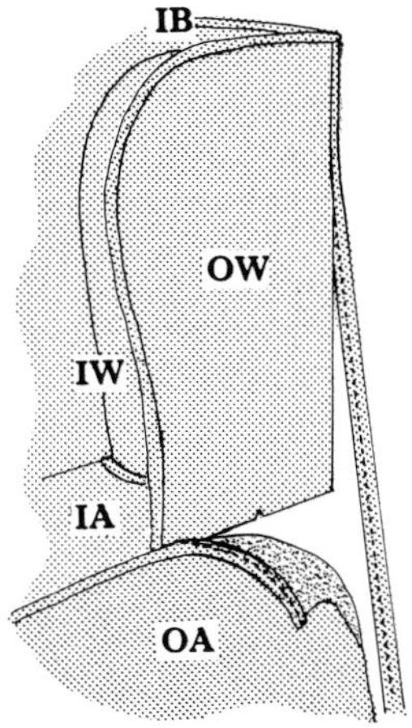

Fig 79

You are now ready to finish joining the Outside Back to the Outside Arms, although this can only be done on one side because you will be fitting the zip on the other side. On the opening side, pin the length of piping previously left hanging on to the Outside Wing and Inside Arm (Figure 81). Neaten the edge and then pin and sew in the zip as for the bedroom chair (page 25).

The base of the chair is taped back using 1.25 cm. (½ in.) tape in the same way as for the loose seats (page 11).

After making a hem on the bottom edge, thread a length of tape through the hem leaving enough to enable you to pull it over the legs and make a bow to tie it up. (Figure 82)

Fitting

Press the cover and fit it on, slipping the Back over first and then the Arms. Tuck it in all round, zip it up and then tie it very tightly underneath. Turn all the pipings to make a sharp line (page 29).

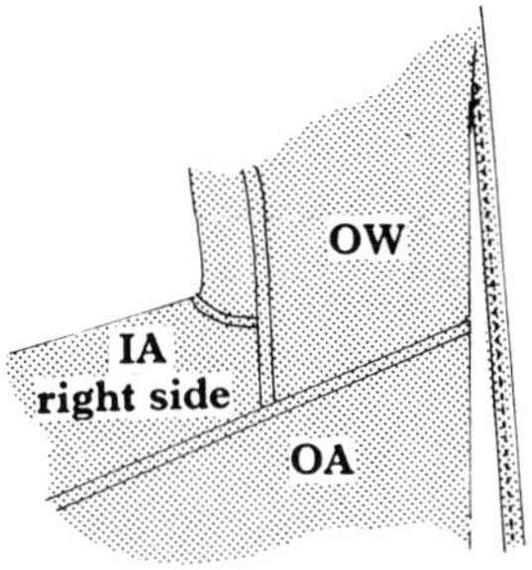

Fig 80

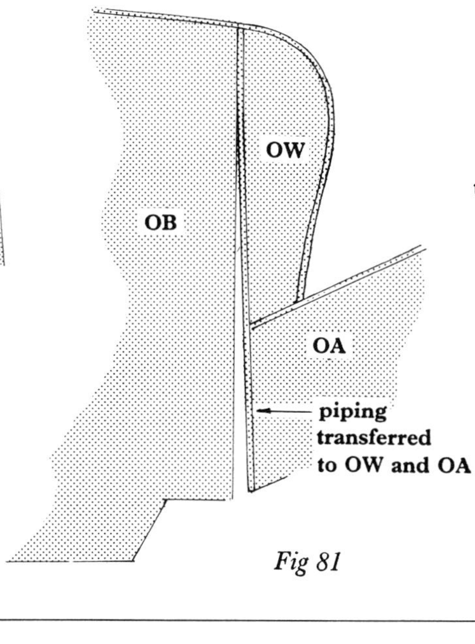

Fig 81

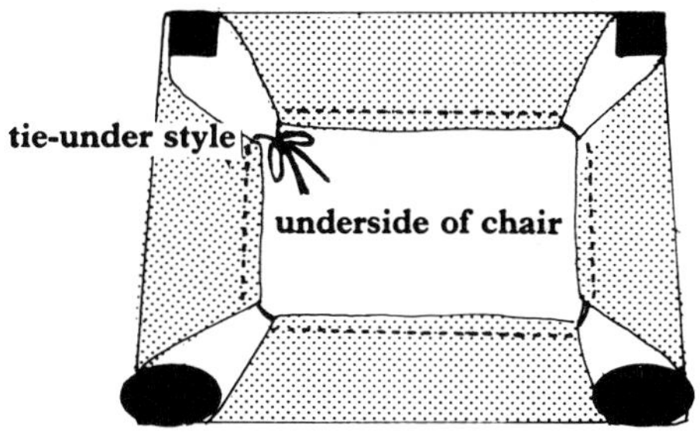

Fig 82

4 Cushions

Cushion Pads – Soft Fillings

Before making the cushion of your choice, it is a good idea to look around and see what ready-made shapes of cushion pads are available. There are quite a few sizes to choose from and sometimes it is more economical to buy a ready-made pad. This, of course, only applies if you want a standard shape as anything unusual or over-sized will cost a good deal more, if it is obtainable at all. It is useful, therefore, to know how to make your own pads.

The case should be cut 1.25 cm. ($\frac{1}{2}$ in.) larger than the finished measurement of the outer cover, plus the usual turnings of 1.25 cm. ($\frac{1}{2}$ in.) on each edge. If you are making a heart shape or any other non-standard shape, draw it on a piece of paper first to the finished size and then, if you are satisfied with the result, pin the paper to the fabric, adding the extra allowance and turnings. (Figure 83)

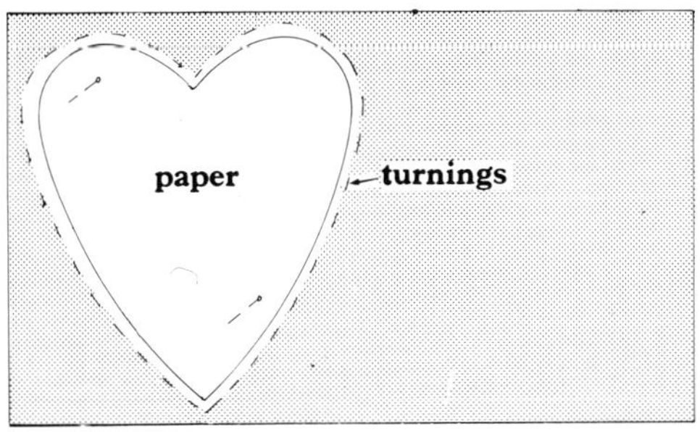

Fig 83

Basically all you need to remember is that the inner pad must be made slightly larger than the outer cover, if it is to have a soft filling. If you use feathers, down or kapok you will need to use a waxed or downproof cambric for the case. Polyester fillings or crumble foam can be used with a strong cotton or lining fabric.

For any square or round shape, measure it out on the fabric – allowing for turnings – and mark the outline directly on to the material with a pencil or tailor's chalk.

Cut out the shape – the fabric can be cut double on these inner cases – and place the two right sides together. Pin all round.

Start machining about a third of the way in from the corner and sew all round, stopping about a third of the way in from the last corner, thus leaving a gap in which to fill the pad (Figure 84). With a round or irregularly shaped pad leave a large enough gap to put your hand in easily.

Sew round again, about half-way along the turning, to prevent any leakage of the filling. (Figure 85)

Turn the pad the right way round, fill with the chosen type of filling and machine the gap by folding in the turning allowance and top stitching along the edge. Fasten off (Figure 86). The pad is now ready for its outer cover.

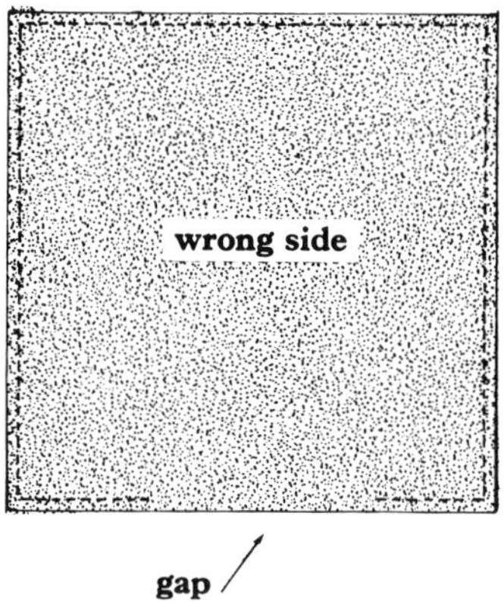

Fig 84

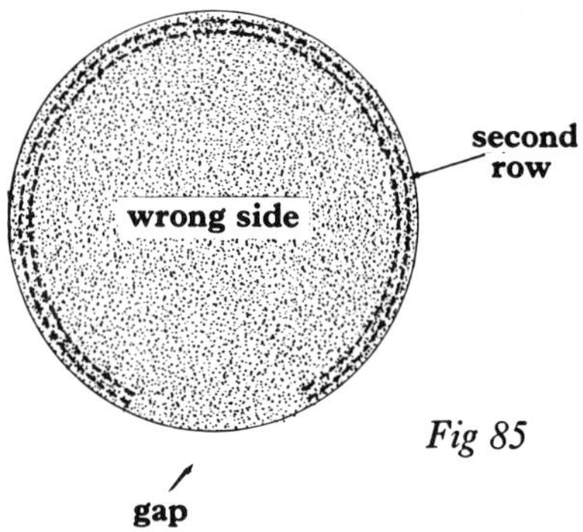

Fig 85

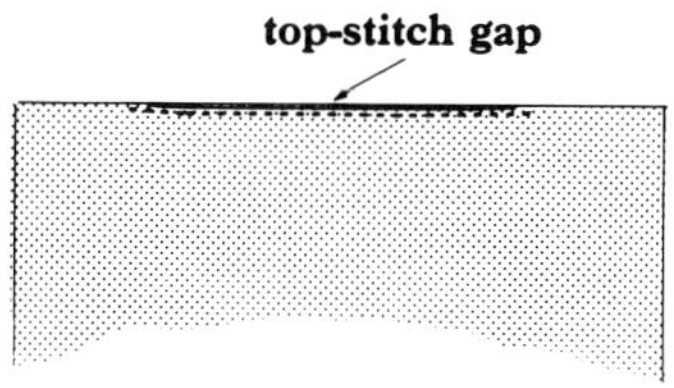

Fig 86

Bordered Cushions

Square shaped – This type of bordered cushion can be used as a back cushion or, if it is cut to fit the shape of a chair seat, almost the same method is used as for the smaller version. The only major difference is that the opening will be at the top of the pattern or at the back of the cushion, on the seat version, whereas all back cushions have the opening at the base or bottom of the pattern.

Cutting out – Measure the inside pad of the cushion you are going to cover (Figure 87). If it has a soft filling, that is to say feathers, down or kapok, the outer case will have to be *smaller* than the inside pad. The reason for this is that, if the pad fits tightly into the outer case, all the corners are pushed out and the filling looks "plump". If the pad is smaller than the outer case, however much it is filled it will always look "saggy".

Instead of the usual practice of allowing a 1.25 cm. ($\frac{1}{2}$ in.) turning on all the edges, therefore, add the turning on one side only (Figure 88). Thus, as the turnings are made during the making up, the outer case will become 1.25 cm. ($\frac{1}{2}$ in.) smaller than the pad.

Fig 87

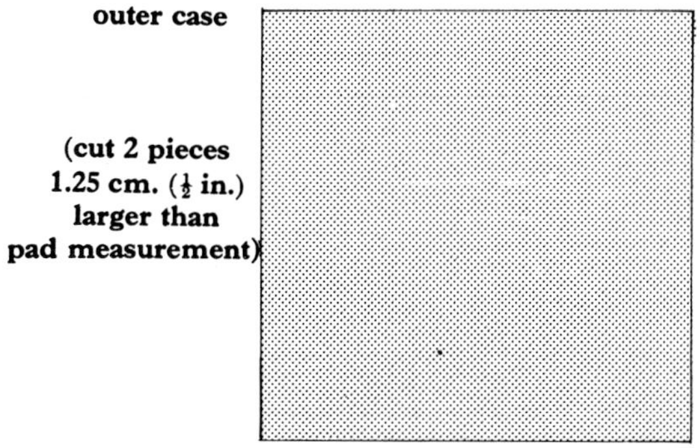

Fig 88

In the case of any type of hard-filled cushion, i.e. hair, rubber, etc., that retains its own shape, turnings of 1.25 cm. ($\frac{1}{2}$ in.) on each edge must be allowed in the usual way.

Cut the cushion cover out by first finding the centre of the pattern; now place a pin at the centre and measure equal distances either side of the pin to give the overall cut size of the cushion. (Figures 89 & 90)

If you do not have a pattern, cut a snip in the selvedge edge and pull one of the threads across the width. Cut along the gap made by the removal of the thread and you will have a straight line to guide you.

However, not all fabrics are so easy to treat in this way as they do not always run square, i.e. chintz and sateen lining. The best method to use for these is to place the selvedge edge on a level with the side of the table top and, on the other edge, draw a line level with the table edge, meeting the selvedge at the corner to give you an exact square corner. Take the measurement required from these edges and the cover will be square. (Figure 91)

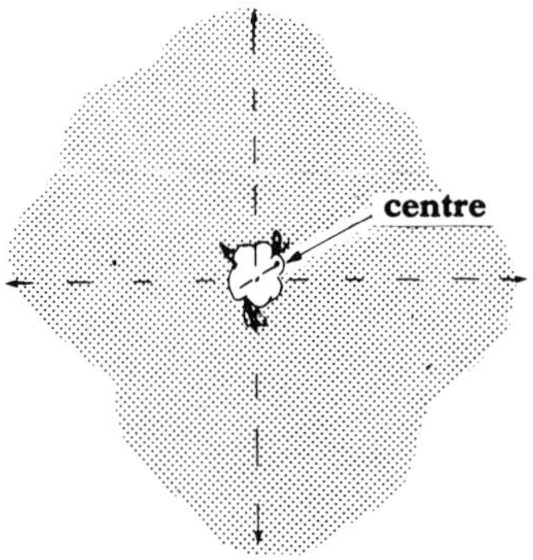

Fig 89

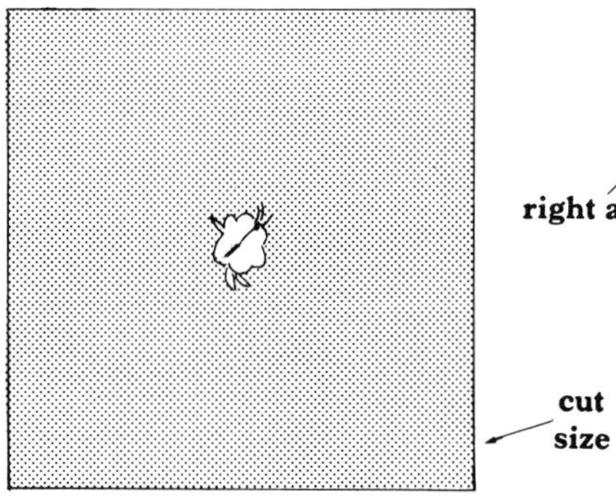

Fig 90

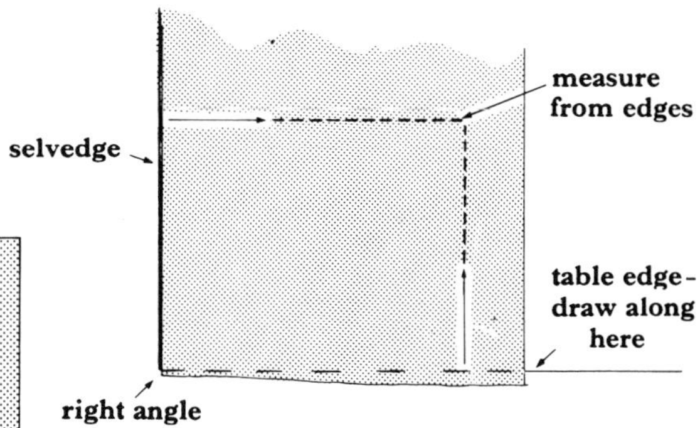

Fig 91

Once the top has been cut, pin it on to the length of fabric and again make sure that the edge is square or, if patterned, match the pattern by placing it on the top. Usually one top and bottom of a cushion can be cut from a width of fabric. With a very small cushion, it is worth trying to get one pattern on the front and a different one on the back; this particularly applies if you are making more than one cushion. If you are able to match two fronts and two backs it is far more economical than taking a centre for every cut. (Figure 92)

Measure the size of the border on the cushion pad, this time allowing the turnings of 1.25 cm. ($\frac{1}{2}$ in.) on both sides. Measure all round the outer edge of the cover and cut a width of border to this size; the depth will be the shorter measurement and the width will be the longer as the border should run upright.

If you are going to put a zip in the border, measure three sides only and cut to size. Now measure across the base of the cover and cut a width this size by the border depth *plus* an extra 2.5 cm. (1 in.). This will give you turnings so that the border can be split along its width to allow the zip to be inserted. (Figure 93)

If you have a patterned fabric, make sure that the border runs in line with the top and bottom of the cushion.

Cut out the piping from the left-over pieces of fabric and cut these across the grain as explained on page 19.

You are now ready to start sewing.

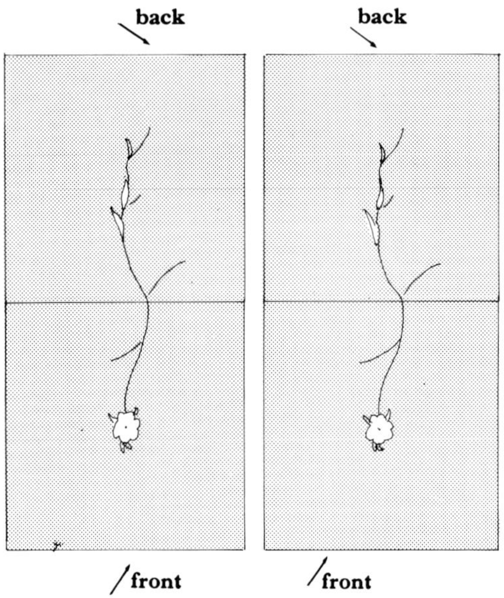

Fig 92

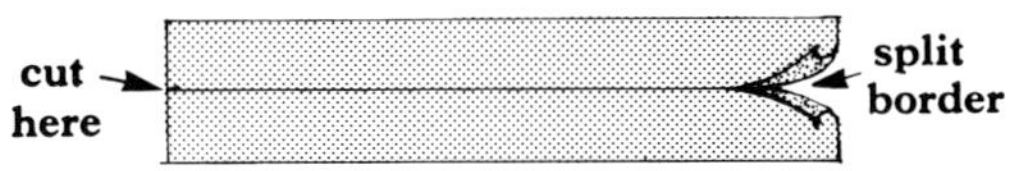

Fig 93

Sewing the cover – First join all the pieces of piping and make a strip long enough to go round the top and bottom with an overlap of approximately 7.5 cm. (3 ins.) on each (page 20).

Starting with the front of the cushion cover, place the piping at the base, half-way across, and pin into place towards the corner.

To turn the corner, cut into the turning on the piping at an angle from the corner (Figures 94 & 94A). Turn the piping sharply and continue pinning round until you get back to the start. Let the piping overlap by 5 cm. (2 ins.) and then cut it off.

Machine all round, leaving at least 7.5 cm. (3 ins.) unsewn at the start and finish.

Repeat this process exactly for the bottom of the cushion cover.

Joining the piping – This needs to be done so that no join is really visible. Pull the lengths of cord out of the way temporarily and place the ends of the piping together. Place a pin across the two ends of piping to close the gap and trim the excess off on either side, leaving a turning of 1.25 cm. ($\frac{1}{2}$ in.) on each piece. (Figure 95)

Open up the piping and, taking the top corner of one piece, place it at the bottom corner of the other piece. Holding these two corners together, pin across the angle to make a cross join. (Figure 96)

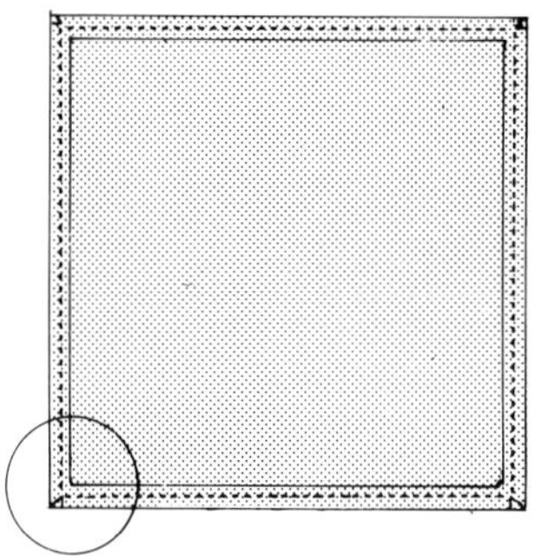

Fig 94

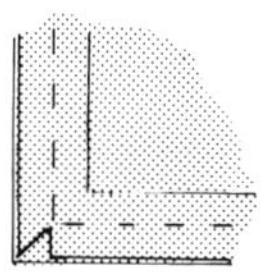

Fig 94A

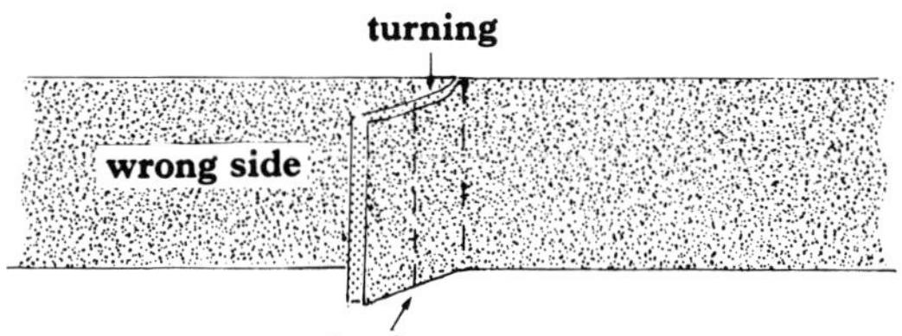

Fig 95

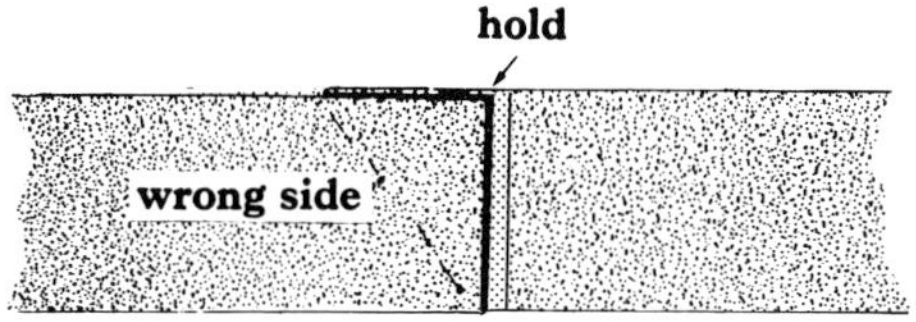

Fig 96

Before machining across, try it to make sure the piping fits the gap. If it is correct, machine across, if not adjust it until it is correct. Trim the turnings across, and open them out flat.

Now place the two lengths of cord side by side so they pass each other, pull the piping so that it fits the gap and then cut right across the two pieces of cord (Figure 97). They will then butt against each other inside the piping. Turn the piping over and continue machining it to the cushion cover.

The join should now be very hard to detect.

After the piping has been joined and sewn into place, the zip has to be fitted into the border.

Fitting the zip – Zig-zag or neaten the two cut edges on the split border and fold back the turning. Press this fold so that you have a creased edge. The zip should be long enough to extend over the whole length of the opening, but if the opening is rather long, you can join the border along the crease line, leaving a gap in the middle to accommodate the zip. (Figure 98)

Place the zip with the right side upwards and lay the border on top of it, with the right side of the border facing up. Make sure the centres of the zip's teeth are lined up with the middle creases. Pin either side of the creases so that the machine will just miss the teeth.

Using a zip foot, machine in a straight line to a point just past the teeth; turn and machine across; turn again and machine near to the teeth once more; when you reach the end of the teeth, turn and machine across to return to the starting point. (Figure 99)

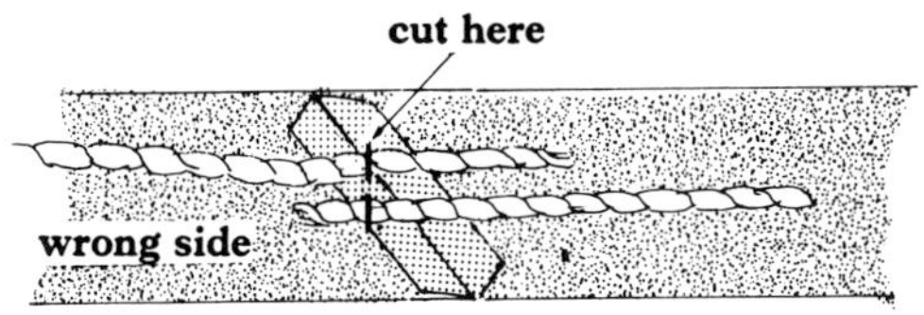

Fig 97

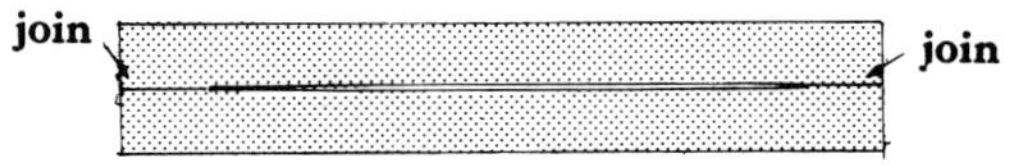

Fig 98

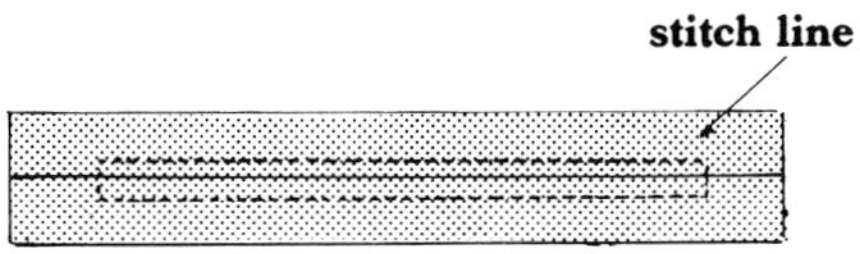

Fig 99

Finish off the machining firmly by reversing over the last few stitches and the zip is now ready. Open the zip a little at this stage because otherwise, when you have finished sewing all round the inside of the cover, you will find that you cannot turn the cover the right way out as there is no opening through which you can undo the zip. (Figure 100)

Attaching the border – Join this piece of border to the other width, so that it forms a continuous band. Pin the top edge of this to the top of the cushion cover, making sure that the pattern runs in line. The pins should be on the cushion side, so that they are easy to remove. If you wish to tack instead, do so at this stage.

Starting from the centre of the base of the cover, machine towards the corner, keeping as close to the cord as possible (Figure 101). When you reach the corner, leave the needle in the work, lift the foot up, turn sharply to make a right-angled turn and lower the foot again, making sure that nothing is caught up on the underside. This method will ensure that you have a good clean corner, without any dragging or pinching of the fabric.

Sew all round in this fashion until you have returned to the beginning. Machine a few extra stitches past the start and fasten off.

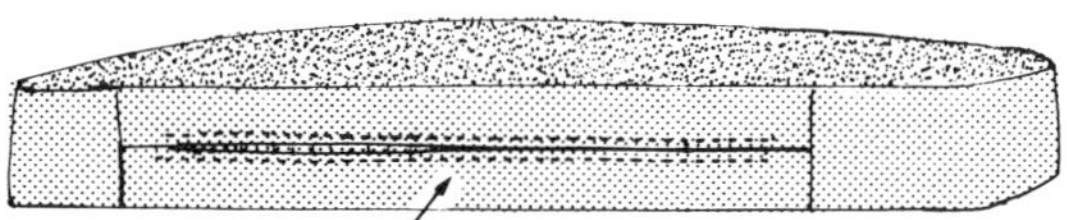

Fig 100

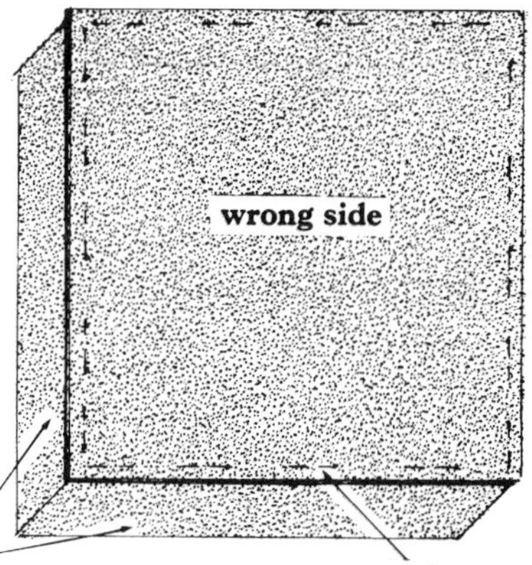

Fig 101

Turn the cover over and join the back of the cushion to the other side of the border, lining up the corners so that they remain upright (Figure 102). The opposite side of the border can be marked with a notch to make lining-up easier.

Sew all round then zig-zag or neaten the edges.

Turn the right way out and press.

To insert the cushion pad, fold the pad in half and push it into the opening as far as it will go; insert your hand into the cushion and work the pad as far as possible into the top corners. The rest of the pad will follow. Push the other two corners into place and zip up the cover. The completed cushion should look just plump but not hard.

Round – This cushion is made in exactly the same way as the square-bordered cushion. The zip is placed in the middle of the border. The circles are piped top and bottom and then assembled to the border. Snip the piping to make it lie smoothly. (Figure 103)

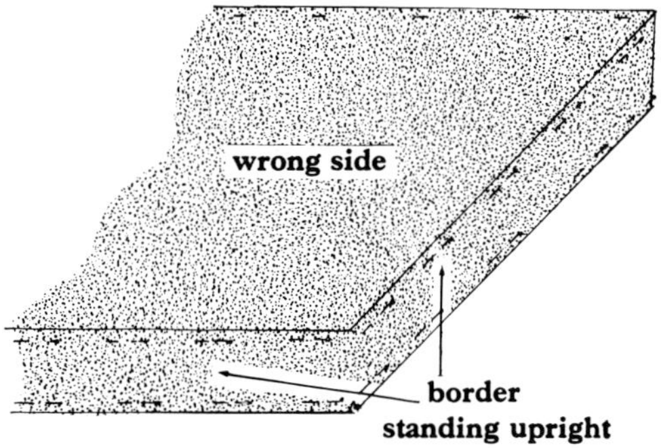

Fig 102

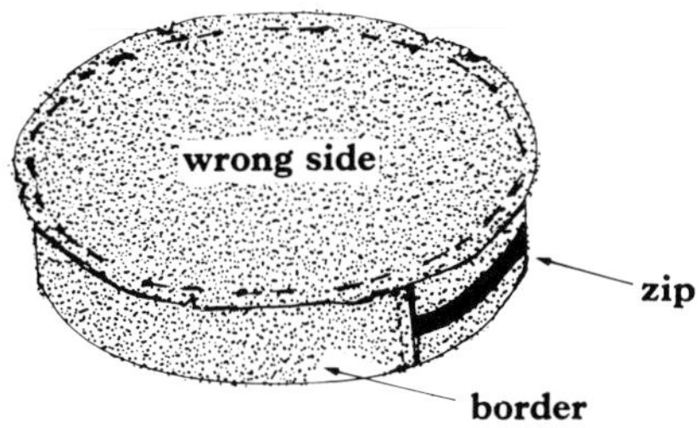

Fig 103

Round with pleated border – Cut out the top and bottom circle and then measure the depth of the border. Now cut enough width of border to go round the circumference of the circle twice. The actual amount of fabric used will depend on how close you place the pleats. To give yourself a guide, pleat up 30 cm. (12 ins.). If you pleat this into a length of 15 cm. (6 ins.), then double the width of the circumference will be enough. If you are being more generous with the pleats and the 30 cm. (12 ins.) pleats down to 7.5 cm. (3 ins.), then you will need to allow three times as much as the circumference.

This cushion will be much neater if it is completely sewn in, so there is no need to allow an extra piece of border for the zip, as was previously done. (Figure 104)

Join the widths of border into a single length; pleat one side by folding the fabric under at even intervals, pinning or tacking into place. (Figure 105)

With practice, this can be done free-hand by machine but, at this stage, it is better to take time and have the pleats really even.

When you have pleated all along one side, turn the whole border round so that, this time, you will be pleating in reverse and the pleats will all lie in the same direction. (Figure 106)

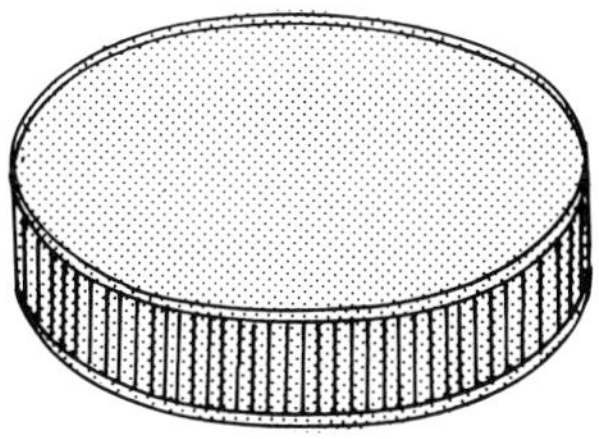

Fig 104 Finished cushion

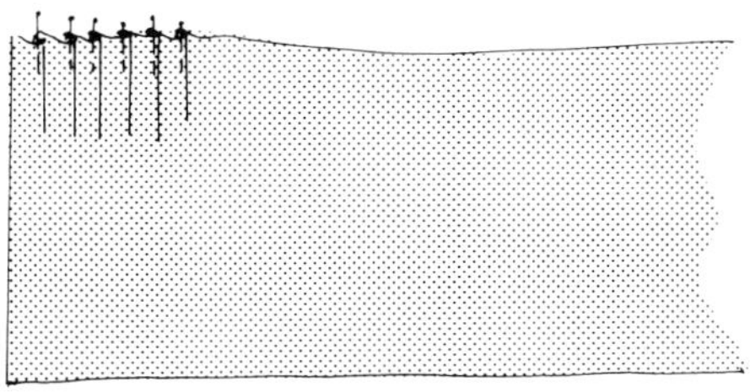

Fig 105

Now that the pleating is ready, pipe round top and bottom circles, then pin pleating into position. Pin the border at intervals all round the top circle, making sure that it fits. Working from the circle side, machine the border to the circle, sewing inside the original row of stitching and as close as possible to the cord.

Turn the cushion over and pin the other circle in place, keeping the pleats upright. Leave a gap of 15 cm. (6 ins.) to insert the pad and sew round the circle in the same manner as the top. (Figure 107)

Sew along the length of piping in the gap, close to the cord; this will mean that, when the cushion is closed, the piping will be the same thickness as the rest.

A variation on the pleating would be to gather the border using the machine gathering technique described on page 27 or to gather by hand.

If this system were to be adopted, the gathers would have to be evened out and pinned into position. The cushion could then be completed as for the pleated border.

Round: pleated top, plain border – This is again a variation, except that this time a button is added in the centre (Figure 108). Although the end result is a circle, a circle shape is not cut out in the first place.

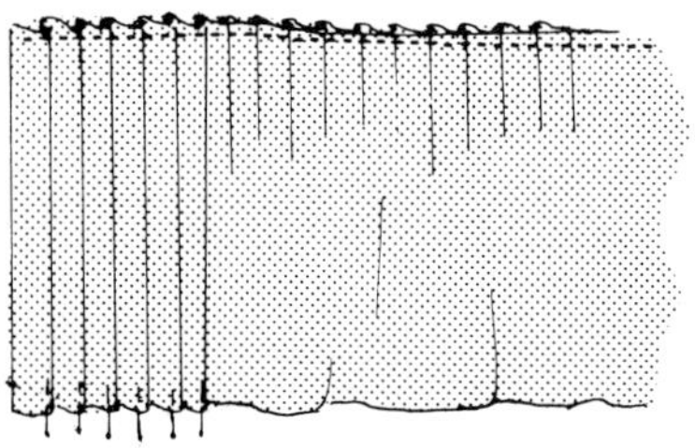

Fig 106

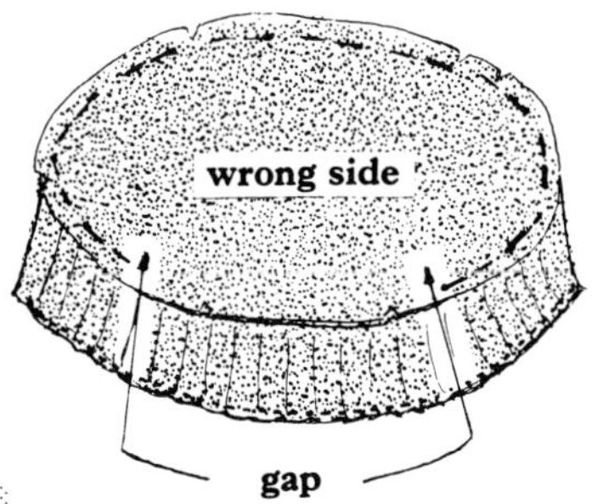

Fig 107

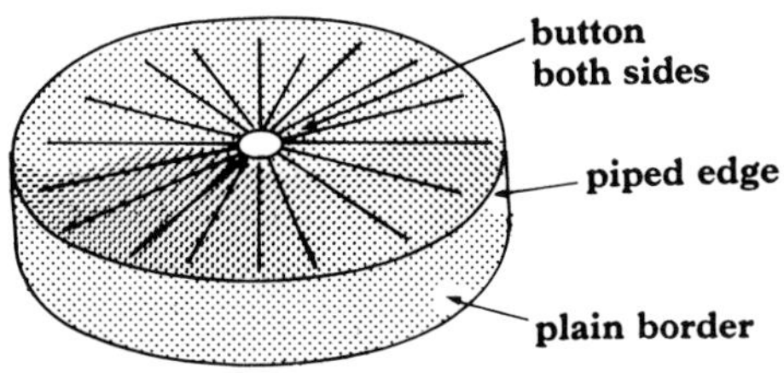

Fig 108

The width of fabric needed for the top and bottom pieces will depend on the size of the finished circle size required. When you have decided the size you require, measure across the diameter; half of this will be the radius and this is the measurement we need (Figure 109). Add to this measurement an allowance for turnings on either side, i.e. a total of 3 cm. (1 in.). This will give you the depth measurement and the width measurement will be the circumference plus 3 cm. (1 in.) for joining. Now cut a strip to these dimensions.

This time the border is cut to fit the size of the circumference of the circle, not forgetting to allow the turnings for joining up.

Join the border into a circle and pipe both edges, joining the piping to complete the circle. (Figure 110)

Join the top strip together and pin the piped border to it.

Machine stitch, keeping close to the cord. Join the strip for the other side and then join this to the border (Figure 111). This time leave a gap wide enough to insert the cushion, when the cover is complete.

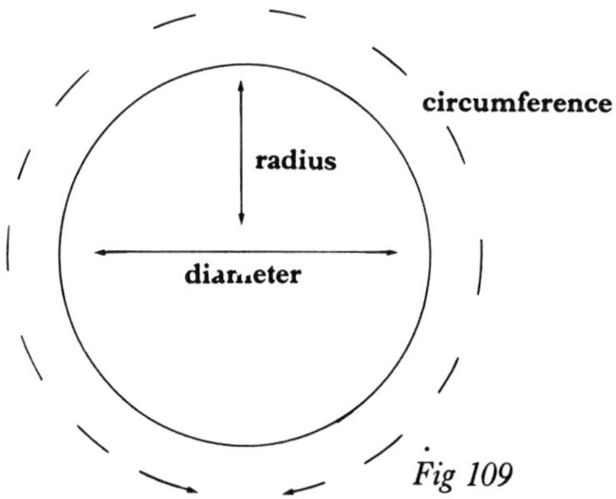

Fig 109

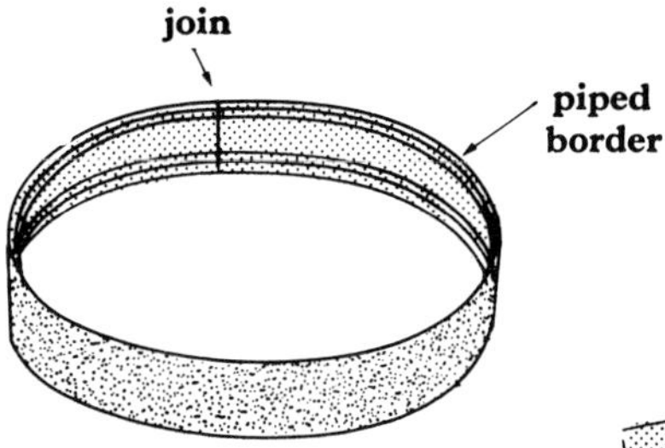

Fig 110

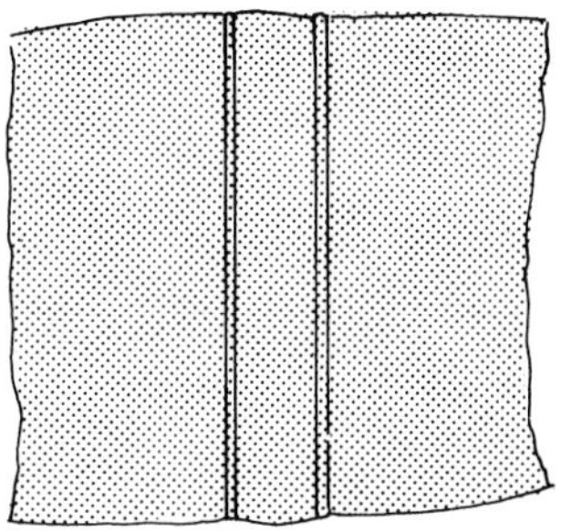

Fig 111 Side view

Using a heavy thread, make a row of stitches all round, just in from the edge of the strip. On the right side the stitch should be 4 cm. ($1\frac{1}{2}$ ins.) long and on the wrong side 0.5 cm. ($\frac{1}{4}$ in.) long. Try to keep these stitches even; adjust them, if necessary, so that they run on evenly where they rejoin at the start. (Figure 112)

Pull the thread up as tightly as possible, so that the bulk of the pleats are on the inside of the cushion, and fasten off the gathering very firmly. Repeat on the other side. (Figure 113)

Insert the inside pad and sew the opening up, using a slip stitch.

To finish the cushion, cover two button moulds – obtainable in any large haberdashery department – 3 cm. ($1\frac{1}{4}$ ins.) in diameter. Using an upholstery needle, or a very long sharp needle, thread the button on to a length of twine, thread both ends through the needle and push it right through the centre hole in the cushion, to emerge dead centre on the other side (Figure 114). Thread the other button on to one of the threads and tie the two pieces together by making a slip knot. (Figure 115)

Pull the slip knot up as tight as it will go so that the two buttons are indented in the centre on either side. Tie the threads off with two extra knots, cut off the ends and the cushion is ready.

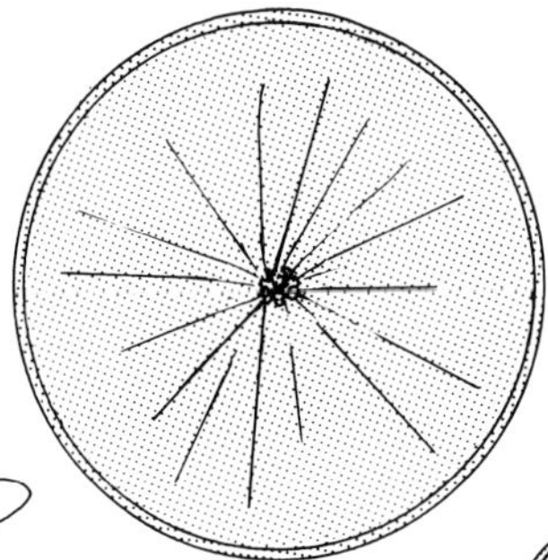

Fig 113

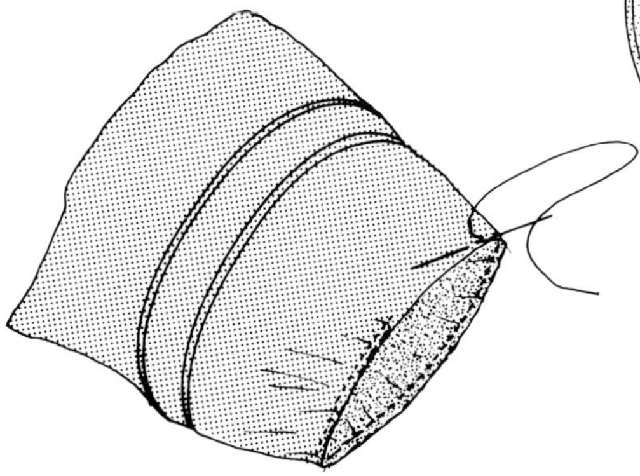

Fig 112

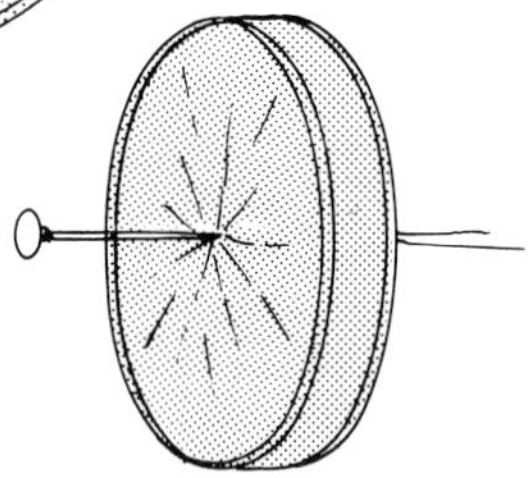

Fig 114

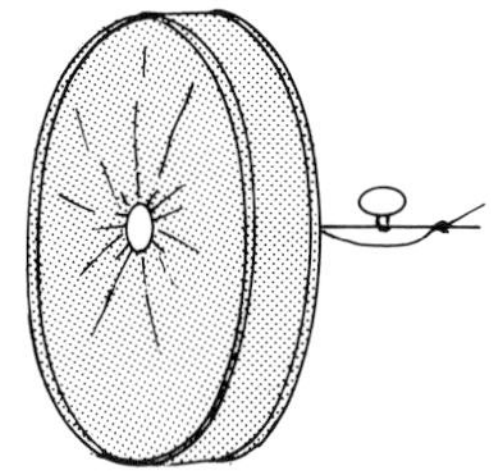

Fig 115

Flat Cushions

These are usually used as back cushions although they are not really flat as the name suggests; it just means that they do not have a border. I have drawn four basic shapes and, as you will see, each one can be trimmed in a different way. You can, of course, experiment with the different styles by varying the colours and trims and by mixing fabrics.

Oblong – Cut out your shape using the methods already described on page 44, allowing for turnings of 1.25 cm. ($\frac{1}{2}$ in.) extra on all sides. Cut a back and a front, matching the centre pattern on both sides, if possible, to produce a reversible cushion.

This cushion is braided and piped as it has a good area to show the braid. The fabric can be patterned or plain. If you decide on a patterned fabric, use one with a small overall pattern or a small centre pattern, so that it can be outlined by the braid and still leave a margin all round (Figure 116). If the fabric is plain, choose a fairly wide fancy braid so that it stands out. (Figure 117)

Only the front of the cushion will be trimmed so that you can reverse it and have a plain back showing instead.

Positioning the braid – Lay the front of the cushion right side up and measure to find the centre. Place a pin exactly at this point. When making your own

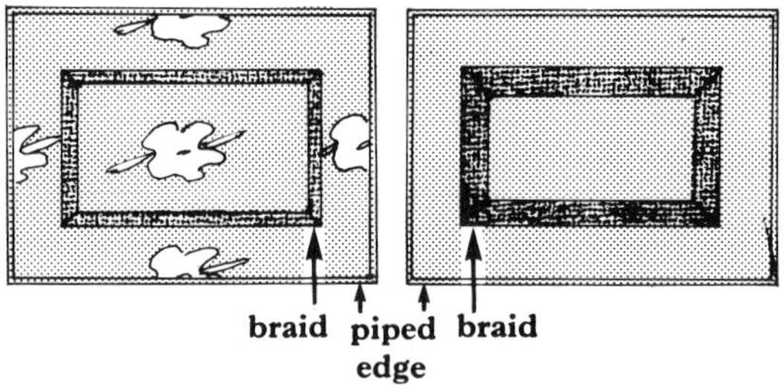

Fig 116/117 Finished cushions

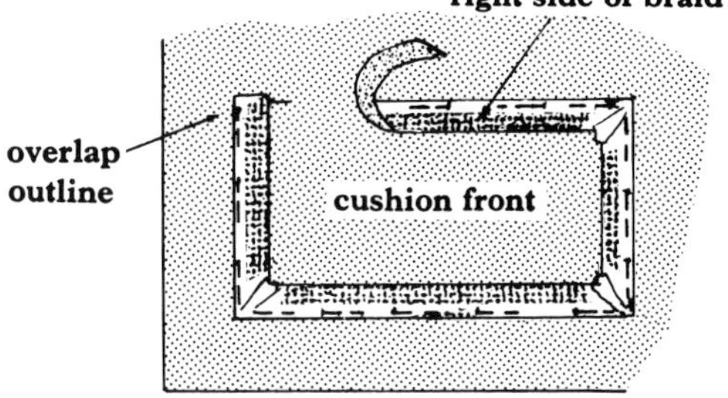

Fig 118

cushion, you would now decide the width of the margin to be left round the edge but our example is going to have an 8 cm. (3 ins.) margin showing. A measurement is therefore taken a distance of 9.5 cm. ($3\frac{3}{4}$ ins.) from the edge and this will give the turning allowance. Draw a line along this measurement and you will have a clear outline to follow. Pin the braid to this line, starting with a slight overlap at one corner.

Pin along to the first corner and turn sharply at the corner point. Continue round until you are at the beginning again, leave a fraction overlapping and trim the braid off. (Figure 118)

Turn under the overlap on both edges so that they meet right on the corner point. Pin into position. (Figures 119 & 120)

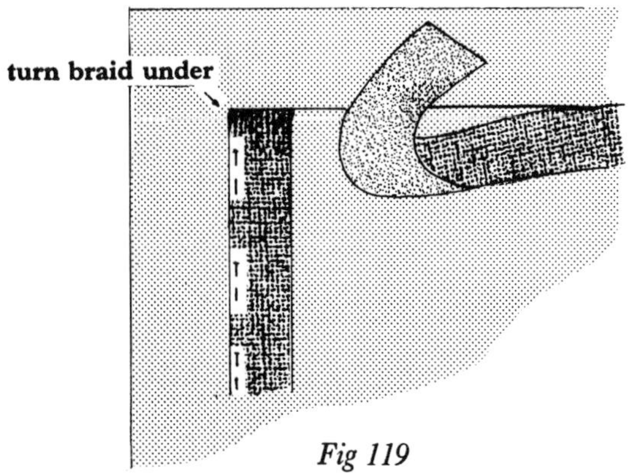

Fig 119

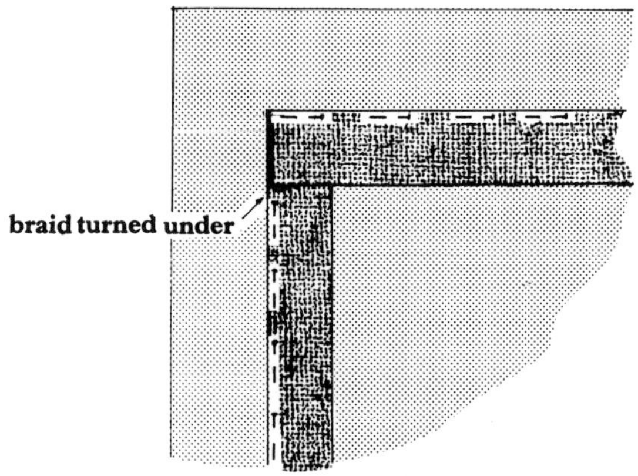

Fig 120

The braid can, with care, be machined in place but if you wish to hand sew it, use a small back-stitch.

Turn the braid under to form a mitre on the corner and pin in place (Figure 121). Continue pinning to the next corner and turn the braid under in the opposite direction so that the mitred corner pairs with the first one. Pin all round and then stitch in place. If the braid is fairly wide, the mitres will need to be slip-stitched down the folds to keep them flat.

Piping – Make up a length of piping and, starting at the centre of the bottom edge, pin it all round, snipping the corners (Figure 122) and joining the two ends as described on page 47.

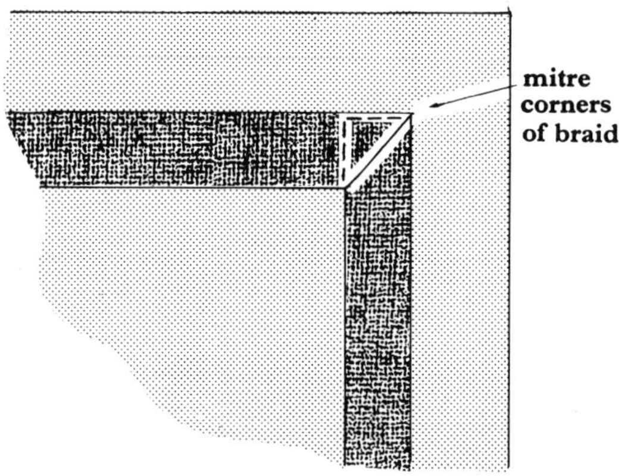

Fig 121

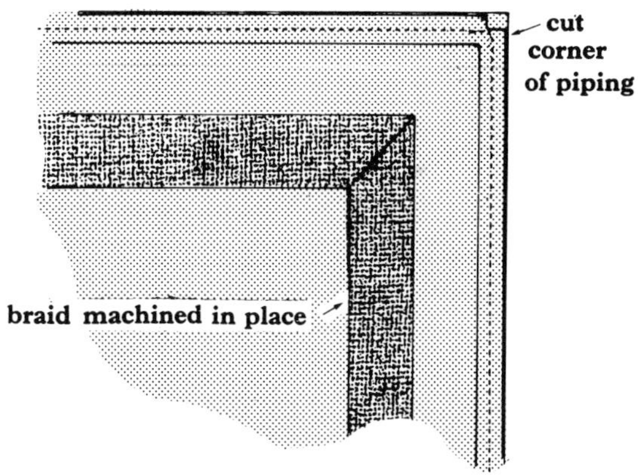

Fig 122

The zip – Having pinned and machined the piping on, the zip can now be fitted to the bottom edge. The zip should be about 10 cm. (4 ins.) shorter than the bottom of the cushion. Place the piped top on the underside of the cushion and join, 5 cm. (2 ins.) in, starting from the corner and working along the bottom edge. Repeat on the other side.

This will leave a gap in the middle in which to fit the zip (Figure 123), following the method given on page 48. Make sure that the top stitching goes in the groove where the piping joins the cushion fabric, as it will then be hidden. (Figure 124)

"*Touch and close*" *tape* – Most of these cushions are neater if the opening is slip-stitched so that it is completely invisible. If you wish to have an opening instead of the zip you can use "touch and close" tape; that is to say, a tape with "burrs", on one length and a fluffy surface on its matching length sold as a pair. A short length of sides 1 and 2, sewn on opposite sides of the cushion opening, gives an excellent closure and, to open, can simply be pulled apart. (Figure 125)

To employ this type of opening, the cushion should be piped on the front side and a length of the tape laid along the machine line of the piping so that it just covers it. Machine in place, as near to the edge of the tape as you can. (Figure 126)

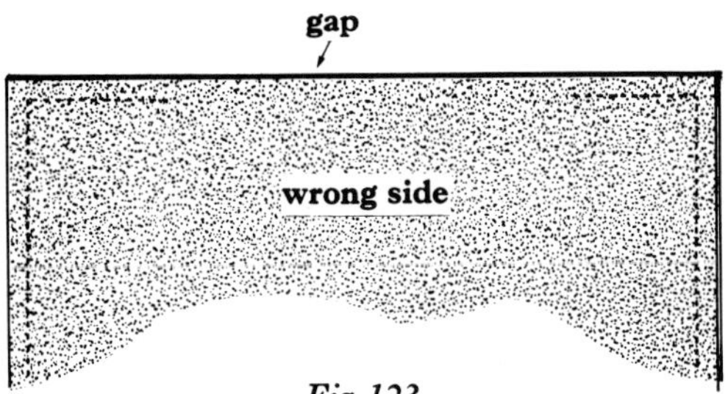

Fig 123

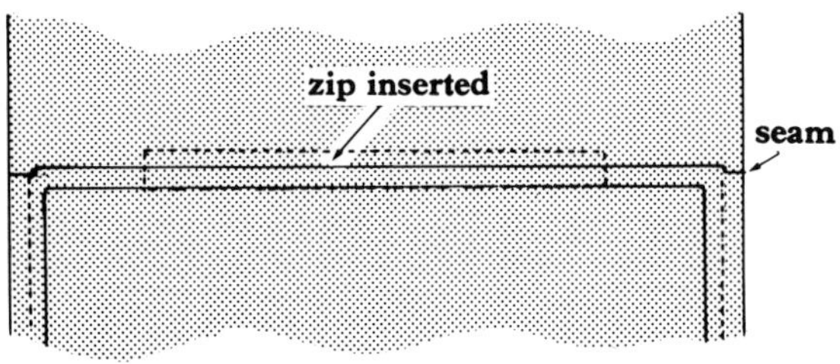

Fig 124

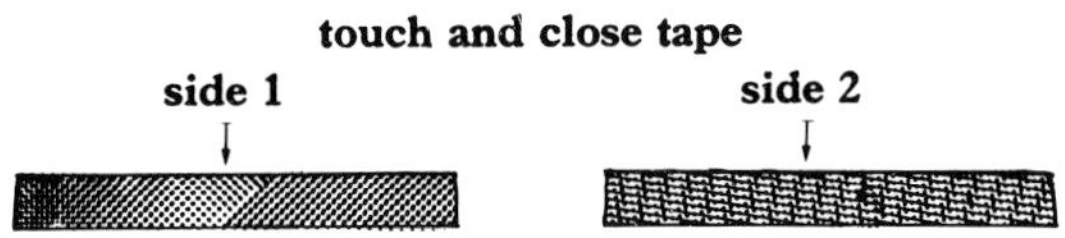

Fig 125

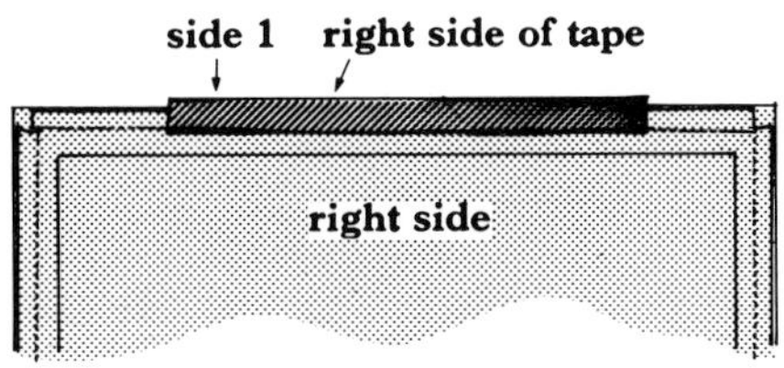

Fig 126

On the other side of the cushion, place the tape so that the edge is in line with the turning fold, right side facing the right side of the cushion, and stitch along this edge. (Figure 127)

Turn the tape over, so that the stitching is hidden. Now continue sewing the cushion all round, from one end of the tape to the other.

Touch the tapes together, so that they are in the correct position, and then sew across, finishing firmly (Figure 128). Neaten all the edges of the cusion inside, open the tape and turn the finished cushion cover the right way out.

Heart-shaped – As lace is going to be used to trim this cushion, the chosen fabric should be a fairly light one, i.e. cotton, chintz or silk.

Cut the shape out in paper to the size you want and then add the turnings. Lay the paper on the fabric and cut both sides.

To trim the middle section, draw a chalk line diagonally across. Leave a gap of 0.5 cm. ($\frac{1}{4}$ in.) either side of the gap and then draw lines at intervals of 2 cm. ($\frac{3}{4}$ in.); four lines each side of the centre mark will be enough. (Figure 129)

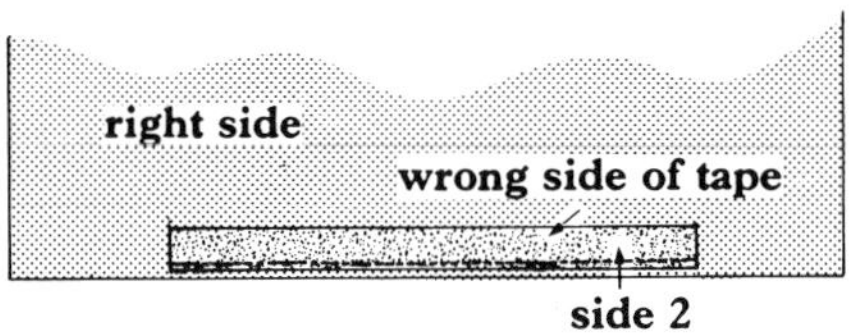

Fig 127

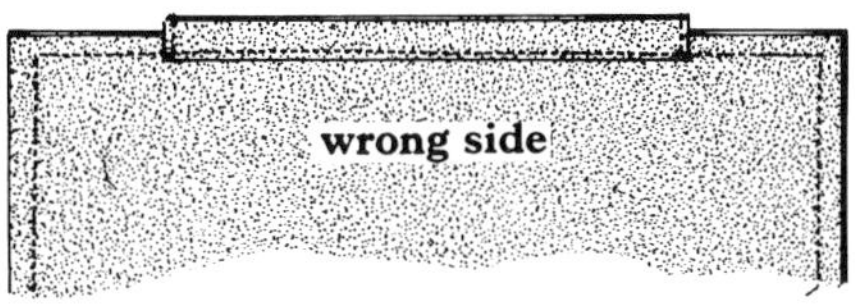

Fig 128

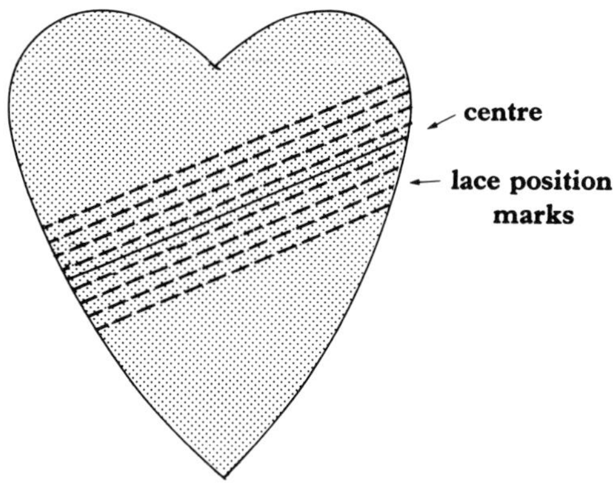

Fig 129

Gather a length of lace along the lower edge and pin it on the line furthest away from the centre line. Machine across the lace at the gathered edge.

Lay the other pieces on and stitch one at a time. Each layer will cover the stitching if you use a 2.5 cm. (1 in.) lace. (Figure 130)

Turn the cushion round and repeat the process, starting from the opposite side. The gap in the centre can now be covered with an insertion lace; this is a flat lace, with holes in it, so that it can be threaded with ribbon. Sew this over the last two pieces of lace, thus hiding the gathers, and thread with a length of contrasting ribbon (Figure 131), leaving enough in the centre to tie a bow.

Using a wider lace, or a broderie anglaise, gather the edge to fit all round the outer edge of the cushion. Make a join where the two ends meet with a neat seam. Pin the lace with the right side facing the right side of the fabric and machine all round the turning allowance.

Place the front and back of the cushion together and sew all round, leaving a gap halfway along the side to insert the cushion. Snip the curves and the top point, so that the fabric will lie without dragging (Figure 132), neaten the turnings and turn the right way out. (Figure 133)

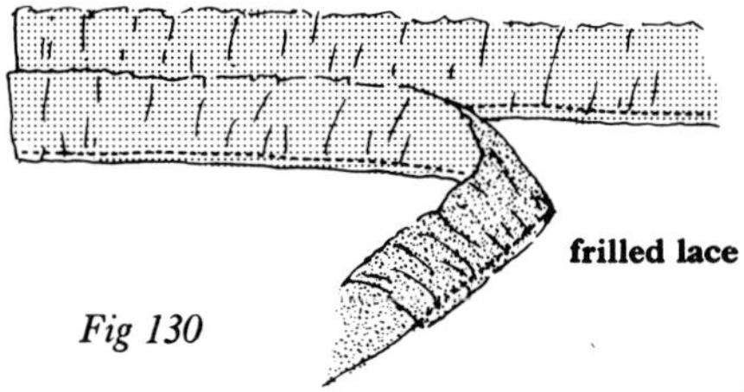

Fig 130

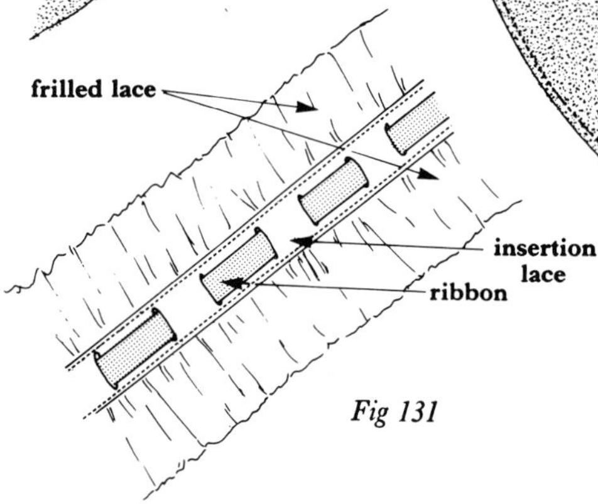

Fig 131

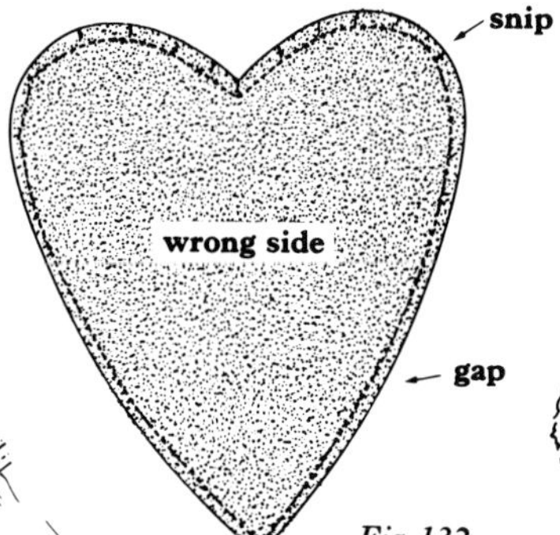

Fig 132

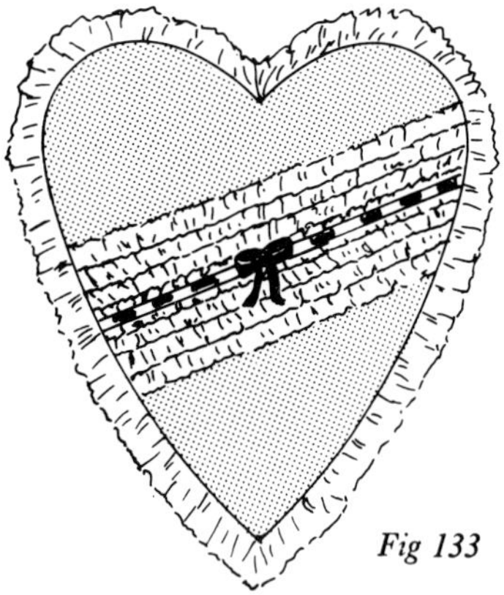

Fig 133

Round – As cushion is going to be piped first and then have its frill added.

Cut the two rounds for the cushion and then cut enough width of fabric to go twice round the circumference. The frill can be either plain or in a small print as there will be a right side of the fabric on both sides. The depth of the frill, therefore, will be twice the finished depth plus the turnings. When you have cut the frill, join it in one complete circle and fold it down the middle lengthways. Gather the raw edges using the machine or hand method described on page 26. Now mark the half and quarter sections, both on the cushion and on the frill (page 27), and gather the frill to fit. Pipe round the cushion in a contrasting colour and then pin the gathered frill in place, keeping all the raw edges together. Machine through all the thicknesses, keeping as close to the piping as possible. Place the front side on the underside of the cushion and stitch round, leaving a gap to insert the pad (Figure 134). Neaten the edges and turn right side out. Insert pad and slip-stitch the opening. (Figure 135)

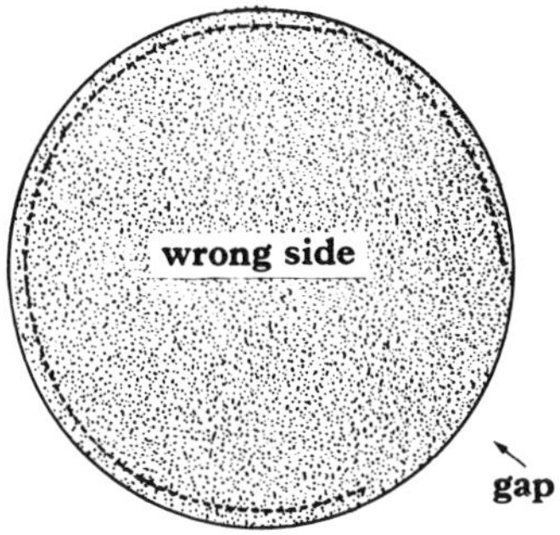

Fig 134

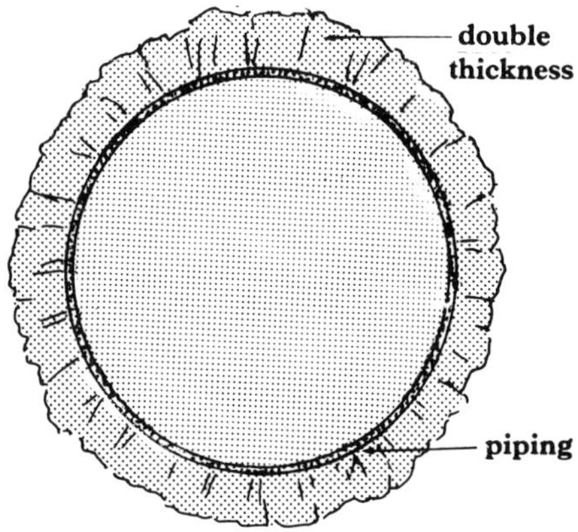

Fig 135

The Triangle Shape

This can be made with odd pieces, like patchwork, using the same fabric in different colours. The back of the cushion can be made in one piece and is cut out first (Figure 136). Now join three pieces of fabric together, roughly forming the shape of a triangle. Place the back on this and cut to shape. (Figure 137)

For this cushion we will make a double frill, with an embroidered edge. Cut the frill to the finished size plus the turnings, and cut enough width to go round the outside twice. Join the frill into a circle. Repeat this again in a different coloured fabric, but make the depth one third shorter.

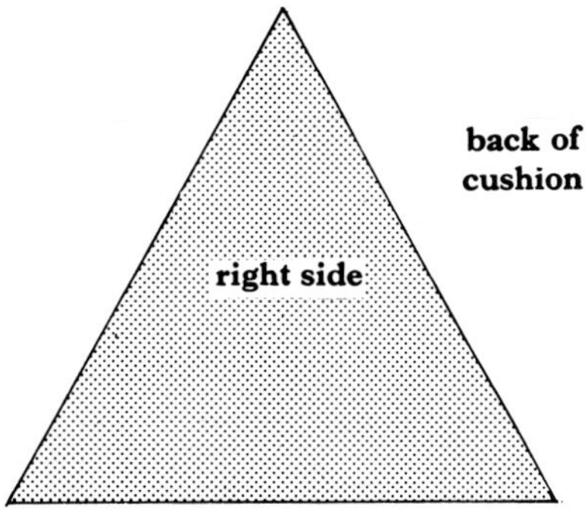

Fig 136

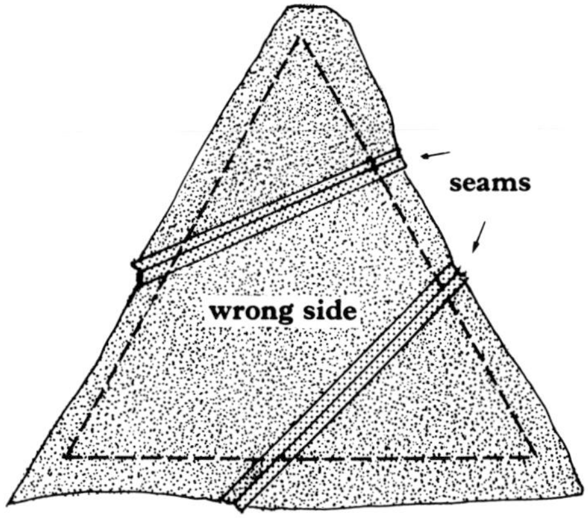

Fig 137

On the raw edge, use one of the machine embroidery stitches to give a fancy edge; the use of a darker colour than the fabric can be most effective (Figure 138). Embroider the edges of both frills (Figure 138) then, keeping the lower edges together, gather them to fit the cushion. Sew on to the front side of the cushion, giving extra fullness at the corners.

Join the front and undersides together, leaving an opening down one side. Neaten and turn inside out. (Figure 139)

There are so many variations, sizes, shapes, colours and methods of decoration that I have been able to give you only a few. I do hope they will encourage you, though, to think up your own individual ideas and that you will be inspired enough to produce some really original work. Loose covers and cushions can give a completely new character to a room, and the possibilities of colour and style are infinitely wider when you have mastered the art of making your own.

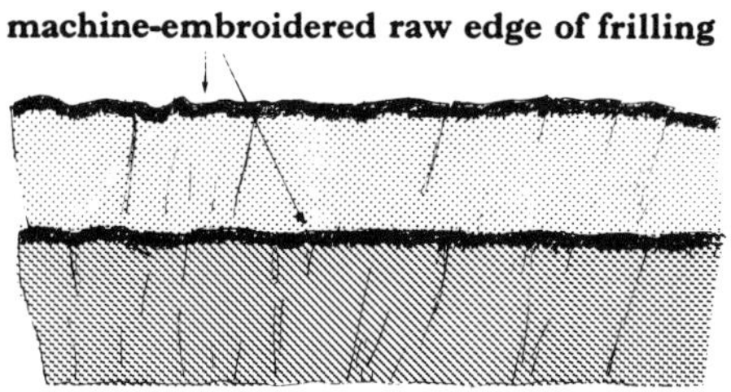

Fig 138

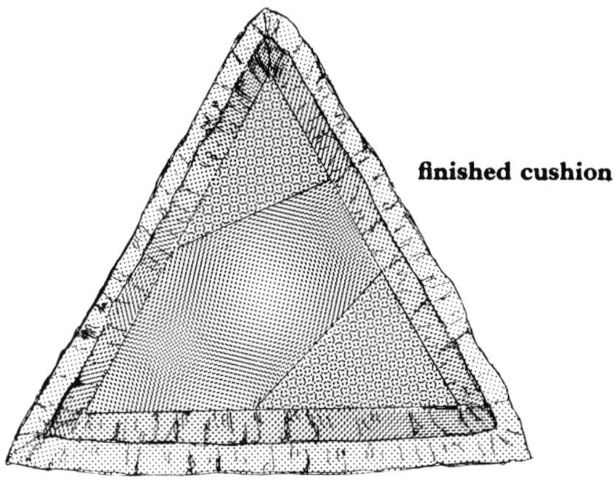

Fig 139